A Sweet Breath of Life

of Life

Transformation

Luzanne Lucas

ACKLOWLEDGEMENTS

To H Lee Barnes – author, creative writing professor and friend. Your critique to personalize it steered me in the right direction. Yes, it took awhile to reprogram my writing mind-set. Thanks so much.

My gratitude to Janet Wellington, editor and a very special lady. "True-blue", always ready with suggestions and practical help, always there with encouragement and support.

To my daughter, Suzanne, computer and format wizard – I couldn't have done it without your expertise. I am pleased and value all you have done, and especially, you are so smart. I am blest.

A basket of "once in a lifetime" peaches to Paula Robins to express my appreciation for your help and support in my endeavor – my first daughter and an avid reader who finds my writing "lyrically expressive". I am twice blest.

And to my granddaughter, Emily Robins, sweet of face and kind heart, whose unintended contribution with words that sing makes forgiving easy. (pg. 59)

DEDICATION

To My Mom

And steadfastly she did strive
to create a better life,
rise above a humble start,
free the sorrow in her heart.

And ever in awe of all creations,
inspired,
she journeyed through life
– undaunted

To Paula and Suzy

and

To Emily

If nothing ever changed, there would be no butterflies.

A
SWEET
BREATH
OF
LIFE

Transformation

Luzanne Lucas

SweetBreaths

CONTENTS

INTRODUCTION

The Seed

On a cool morning in the second week of second grade, after the pledge of allegiance, there came a knock, knock, knock on the classroom door. Upon answering and speaking in hushed tones with the visitor I could not see, our teacher then came to my desk. My classmates stared. Flustered, I could barely raise my head when she told me to get my sweater and come with her.

In the hallway stood a tall lady dressed in a dark uniform and strange looking hat. "We are going to see the principal," she said. While we walked side by side in silence, an awful feeling came over me. Even at that young age, somehow I knew I would never forget this day.

Entering the principal's office, I was surprised to see my mother and rushed to her side. She hugged me and told me not to fret, everything would be okay. The principal interrupted to say my mother wasn't well and until she was able to take care of me, I would be placed in a children's home. "Lots of children to play with there," he added. I wanted to cry, but couldn't.

The Social Services lady told my mother, if she felt well enough, she was welcome to ride with us on the long drive to the home. My mom really didn't look well.

We sat in the back seat, my hands in hers. Now, my tears began to flow. She held me close and said I must be

1

brave, soon I'd be coming home and we would be together again. After awhile, she leaned her head back and closed her eyes.

But I didn't feel like being brave. Already, I was missing her. Especially, I'd miss our special times together. While we rode in silence, I comforted myself with this memory. I could almost hear her calling to me . . .

"Come!" she'd say, "it's time to rest. Come! Let's take some sweet, deep breaths and rest."

In a wink, I'd leave the imaginary friends I invited for tea or other magical gathering little ones can so easily conjure and run to her, my open arms eager for her warm embrace.

She'd prepare a refreshing drink for us and we would sit at the kitchen table or, when the weather was nice, on the back porch steps overlooking the plentiful garden, the sour cherry tree, the giant hollyhocks so colorfully camouflaging an old wooden fence. And once I had settled down, in a thoughtful manner she would say, "Let's take some deep breaths; let's pay tribute to our breath of life."

Ceremoniously inhaling "all the air of the universe", puffed up like a young puffin, I'd hold my breath until I thought I might simply burst! I loved hearing the comforting sound of her laughter expressing sweet approval of my breathtaking performance. I basked in her pleasure of me. Then, as her laughter grew quiet I'd follow her lead, taking deep breaths while sharing good thoughts and feelings. And when it was time for her to return to mundane things, I'd secretly wish I could have her all to myself much longer, doing things together.

Yes, already I was missing her and hoped with all my might she would soon get well.

On the incline leading to the entrance of the home, a massive place that held a large red brick building and four smaller ones I could see, again the bad feeling crept over me.

After a short conversation with the administrator, my mom hugged and kissed me goodbye.

And then, she was gone.

Robotic-like, obediently I followed the matron who led me to my new "home". And like a robot, I was known as "5-25" for 40 girls or more of pre-menstrual age were assigned to Cottage #5.

But the Fates weren't kind. Seven long years had to pass until we were destined to be together again. Once more I felt the comfort of her warm embrace and heard her say, "It's time to rest and take some sweet breaths of life."

When that day came, I looked into her face with the magnetic eyes and radiant smile thinking how nice that something so simple could make her feel so good. And my thoughts returned to a time when I was very small and life seemed sweeter, and we were doing something together.

Not for years to come did I comprehend the essential meaning of my mother's words, nor in my wildest dreams imagine this childhood memory would be my saving grace. Or, even be the seed of inspiration for *A Sweet Breath of Life*.

* * *

I have shared two childhood happenings with you to illustrate the way events in our young lives hurt or inspire us – how they help to create who we were and influence who we become.

On this transitional journey, I will help you uncover the hidden ways yesterday's teachings and experiences can govern thinking, control the emotions, even decide the choices you make. You will see what lies beneath the surface that stirs up trouble and gives energy to a spiritless you, an unfulfilling life. And, quite possibly, for the first time ever, you will see why you have become who you are.

To begin, I invite you for a passing visit through the meandering years I once wandered, so you can know I understand where you are coming from and how I came upon the insight to make the necessary changes needed.

My objective is *A Sweet Breath of Life* will be the inspiration to experience a happier life for you as well.

PART I

A Sweet Breath of Life

"Oh, Dear, What Can the Matter Be?"

Among my memories, I see a troubled me in search of something missing from my world, *my soul.*

And in this hoodooed place of discontentment, I turned to a variety of inspirational books and audios for encouragement and help. Like a tyro thirsts for knowledge, in great anticipation I'd devour each "companion" hopeful its message would put to an end my hunger for happiness.

But there was never enough.

I'd be inspired for a day or two, perhaps a week, and then poof! Gone! The words of wisdom unremembered, the inspiration no longer inspiring. And like a chronic ill, my disquieted soul would rise again to remind me that the "placebo" just didn't work.

One day when I was feeling especially blue, I happened to look at the collection on the book shelves and wondered, "Are other people's libraries like mine? Are they, too, searching? Seeking the elusive something to fill the void within?"

Scanning the cover titles, I noted I had been open-minded in my quest for on the shelves an impressive assortment of inspirational, spiritual, philosophical and self-help books stood in silent testimony.

To mention just a few, among them were the writings of mythology by Joseph Campbell, the exceptional philosophy of Ayn Rand, the delightful *Importance of Living* by Lin Yutang and, of course, *The Power of Positive Thinking* by Norman Vincent Peale. I noted the Bible, Missal, Science and Health, and other religious teachings I had delved into. I mustn't overlook the metaphysical musings of astrology, revealing why one is as one is, why others are as they are, or the timing of events in one's lifetime. And how could I forget the many little books of wisdom held atop of and inside the night stand by my bed?

On the shelf below sat my jumbo maroon stationery box with secret pull-out drawer, a treasured gift from Santa many Christmases ago, now filled with an assortment of audio tapes created expressly to raise one's level of consciousness. Among them were those from a seminar I attended, so eager to learn the "proven method" for achieving gratification and success.

As instructed, I'd repeat the affirmations promising to transform my ordinary thinking into the extraordinary and presto! Life is very good! I played them while driving or taking a relaxing bath and, sometimes, while falling asleep. At work, I played the subliminals, their musical passages orchestrated to penetrate the subconscious with positive thought power, thus releasing fear and worry—or any other negative surplus.

Having driven my self to distraction with all the "stuff" held in my head, I puzzled aloud, as though in doing so my thoughts spoken might divine an answer and give me mental rest. "Why don't the uplifting words, the inspirational thoughts stay? Why won't they work?"

No "light bulb," no epiphany—nothing.

Like times before, there I sat pondering still. Why do I feel incomplete? What is missing from my life? Was it my fate to live in eternal exile from experiencing a happy me?

Resigned, I found consolation in the thought that at least the words read, the voices listened to, would always be with me.

Once again, I was with my emptiness, humming the childhood song, "Oh, dear! What can the matter be?"

I decided it was time to put my quest to rest and accept what life had to offer.

But what did life have in store?

None too soon, I would find out.

An Uncommon Happening

While I had been searching, the years stole away—absconded with my prime of life. Gone! Forever gone.

This particular time found me suffering a setback from a recurring abdominal condition, made worse by a nasty viral bug. And if all truth be told, an emotional cripple from years of unending responsibility, coupled with too much heartache and woe. All by myself, I entertained fated thoughts.

And so, this is how my world was when, in the wee hours of one mid-November day, the unexpected was about to occur. I shall never forget that day. Not ever.

Having a fitful rest and feeling especially queasy, I decided I had better eat *something*. As I was leaving the bedroom to enter the hallway to the kitchen, I became extremely warm and nauseous, my vision blurred, a strange numbness filled my chest. I couldn't breathe. Suddenly, my heart was pounding, now galloping! I tried to reach my bed, although I don't know why. I truly thought I was dying and didn't seem to care. My last awareness was of falling.

From within a place of nothing but black space, so strangely quiet, eerily still, came a voice – at first like a whisper, then loud, louder, "Take a deep breath, a sweet breath of life!"

I seemed to be a child and, once again, my mother and I were doing something together. Could this be happening? How can this be? Where am I?

Again I heard the voice, commanding now, "Take a deep breath, a sweet breath of life!" But no breath would come. There was nothing.

Then in that suspension between sleep and wakefulness, a presence of great energy enveloped me. I was mesmerized.

As though I were looking through a frosted window seeing things unclear, yet there; as though I were being caressed, the presence held me so I might clearly "see". I sensed the presence had feelings. There were flickers of light, pulsing, touching, fading then returning, emitting sounds in rapid, high-pitched, yet muted tones. And while entranced, the breath of life pulsed through my being, awakening my being with great understanding. How did I see the enlightenment?

Like one holds a seed and sees the flower.

I have no sense of how much time had passed when I became aware I had fallen, sprawled against the side of the bed, my head in an awkward position. Cold and disoriented, and seemingly in slow motion, I crawled deep under the covers.

As I lay in bed not fully awake, my frazzled nerves shivering to keep me warm, I held onto what I was now dimly conscious of. Though not a word had been "spoken", I understood many things in a manner hard to explain. Try to imagine all the meaningful learning of your lifetime expressed in a single thought. Try to imagine all the love you have known embodied in a single caress.

11

While enrapt in my mental web, exhausted, I felt myself sinking and as the arms of Morpheus were encircling me, I implored my soul not to let one tiny detail be forgotten or lost from memory.

In late morning, I thought I heard the phone ring. The urgent need to use the bathroom stirred me out of bed.

Glancing into the mirror as I rinsed my hands and face, I wondered, "Is this really me looking into the mirror?" My ghostly, ghastly, image moved me to quickly turn off the light. Still, I questioned, "Am I really here, alive?" My faithful heart, rhythmically beating, told me this was so.

Wobbly and weak, slowly, carefully, I made my way toward the kitchen (again). I filled the teapot, placed it on the burner, then fed my very hungry, very patient cat. I drank a bit of juice, scrounged up some bread and placed it in the toaster. Pop! I buttered the toast and while taking a ravenous bite, tried to recall when I last ate. The kettle's whistle blew. I steeped the leaves laced with sweet-smelling orange spice and with tea and toast in hand, slowly, carefully, made my way back to bed.

While savoring my little repast, the reality of what had happened caught up with me. My thoughts were focused on the awesome experience, examining every detail. I was mesmerized by what I knew and didn't know.

I was certain I had suffered an episode with my heart – the most unexpected (if that can be) of any in the past. Most likely brought on by my viral bug, I reasoned.

I decided the flickers of light were pulsations of neurons arising from the trauma to my being, like when you receive a hard blow and see stars.

I concluded the urgings of my mother's familiar words "take a deep breath" aroused my unconscious; my being somehow knowing the deep-rooted memory would help rescue me from the depths of wherever I had entered. Although I had close calls before, I never heard a voice or experienced such a mind-boggling happening.

As my thoughts grew clearer, the realization I understood things unknown to me removed any suspicion of delirium. I asked myself, "How else would I have the insight to see my way out of a life of discontent? Or, even know what I had spent a lifetime searching for?" It was me! Or, should I say I?

I was missing from my life!

It was clear now. I experienced an epiphany, if you will, in an altered state. A scary and wonderful, just pure and simple, bona fide mystical experience!

I was certain the workings of my mind had made the critical contact, the necessary connection for survival, and the outcome of one's fate may often lie in the delicate balance of this single, yet vital, passage within one's being.

I was certain the "presence" was the energy of my soul and, as incredible as it may seem, had allowed me to observe the interaction taking place within my mind. Though I was often troubled but knew not why, it took the intuitive logic of my soul to identify who and what the trouble was. Imagine! *I* was my trouble!

There was no doubt the revelation came from my inmost being, my soul, and as I grew, everything has been held in its care. Now, I understood. The soul of my being revealed what I consciously didn't want to accept or face.

I knew why the presence had feelings, for my soul is everything I have thought or looked upon; each word I have spoken, heard or read; all the knowledge, learning, and experiences; all my joy and laughter, every tear I have shed, every feeling and emotion I have ever felt; every microscopic detail of my life. I knew my soul is the spirit of every breath I have ever taken, the energy of each breath I was now taking.

And I knew . . . I *am* my soul.

Interim

The thought of calling the doctor and having to go to the hospital for tests didn't excite me. (Been there, done that times before.) Physically, I was very weak from all the "heartfelt" excitement and, too, my viral bug was full-blown now with frequent trips to the bathroom. My mental state, though somewhat in a place of astonishment, was fine—just fine.

For several days the awesome encounter with my being haunted my every thought. Often, I found myself chasing after elusive "somethings" racing through my head. Well, except for the times when my state of abstraction was pre-empted by a sudden waterfall of tears, like a dose of prescribed medication.

Once, as I lay sleeping, I awoke trembling to find my face, my pillow, drenched with tears. *I had been sobbing in my sleep!* The uncontrollable tears continued until dawn, as if a drastic cleansing was essential to wash away any unseen barrier in the way of my escape from exile.

At this time and for days to come I marveled at the subtle change in me – as though I had been rearranged, like a bouquet of yesterday's flowers. And I'd say to myself, "I am different." Often (for hadn't I been remiss for too many years?), I'd take sweet, deep breaths and pay tribute to the energy pulsing life through my being. I still do.

During this time of healing I pondered. "What is the difference that makes me feel different? How can I describe the awareness that now fills my being?" How did I know "I am my soul"? I never imagined my soul's happiness depended on me.

I puzzled, "Why, with all the searching through books and listening to those wiser, hadn't I come upon this insight? Certainly, this has been known by others. How did I miss it? Was I so muddle-headed, dense?"

I needed something tangible. I decided to revisit the happening in a practical, dispassionate manner.

"Like one holds the seed and sees the flower."

Like a parable, the message was clear. I saw the seed but not a flower. Only the seed, me, lay there.

In this way the epiphany revealed what was missing was *me*. When the seed isn't nourished, the yield is nothing, waiting to be "known" or to fade away. When the seed is nurtured, its bloom is bright and beautiful.

This is how I understood what I had to do – such a good feeling knowing where to begin.

I was to return to the past to the "seed" of my beginning and the cause of a "discontented" me would reveal itself.

Oh, the irony! Though I was so sure I was my own person, for my entire life I never gave thought to "who" that person was—the essence of me. Almost every moment of my precious life had been filled with muddled thoughts and diaphanous dreams. It was time to take personal inventory. I began at the beginning, the very first memories of my life.

I wrote my name, birth data, eventful happenings, those who entered my life and my emotional response to each, such as: fear, joy, trust, distrust. I noted my capabilities, likes, dislikes; choices and decisions; I assessed my moral code and values. Some happenings weren't easy to "re-live".

When I had finished some several days later (adding to it as I started feeling better), I was surprised to see I held a dozen legal size pages.

Reading my 'bio' was quite a revelation! Though I couldn't determine the exact cause, I felt the emotions of harsh, early beginnings. I didn't know my alcoholic father, I saw him once at a distance. My mom, most always, was busy working.

Most surprising was my emotional response when I noted the day I went to the children's home – now I felt a sense of abandonment. Reliving the memory almost made me ill. I could see how the teachings and happenings through those years alienated me from my young and vital spirit, thus creating a different me, helping to become the flower I was, or should I say, the flower I wasn't?

The anxiety of verbal or physical punishment had "settled in" and became a pattern. Often accommodating to please and be accepted, my kindness came across as weakness—big, bad demon. Upon realizing I merited little regard and small respect, my deeply felt hurt unleashed a fury like no other—two big, bad demons. This was quite a revelation.

I could see I had some good qualities—reliable, trustworthy and caring—this was nice to know. I could see my faults and weakness, like rushing into the unknown

17

where only fools dare to go — not so nice to know. I learned, too, I wasn't "street smart" or as smart as I thought I was. As I noted my reaction to each, definite patterns began to emerge. The theory of cause and effect did apply to me!

There were more entries I thought of later, and more demons appeared, too. As I wrote literally talking to myself, I found the introspection most gratifying.

Studying my 'bio' I could see the positives. I saw the negatives creating my emotional distress, helping to create my sorrow. I saw the shackles that bound me—those I wrapped around myself and those I allowed others to wrap around me.

Looking beneath the surface, seeing who I'd become, was quite an awakening! Most of all, I saw the culprit causing my lifelong discontent . . . *it was me!* This was enlightenment!

My mind-talk was unhappy talk of trouble and fear; the feelings I transmitted to my soul were of sadness and regret (and crying, lots of crying). Soul could only nurture what it received.

In identifying my "modus operandi" (mode of operating), I was able to see why I became who I'd become. The literal self-discovery gave me a clear vision of who I "really" am. This was an eye-opener! I still have my 'bio', except those for "my eyes only" — they went into the garbage. (Before doing so, I digested what I had written.)

My 'bio' example is your guideline to show you where to begin and how to write your 'bio'. As we travel on you will see why your "life story" is essential to understanding the relationship you have with your soul.

Writing your 'bio' centers you, the result gives you clear and needed insight. You can begin now or at a later time, but you must begin. Do I hear you thinking, "Horrors! I can't write!" Yes, you can. If I can, so can you.

You mustn't allow the fear of facing what you might uncover be the barrier between you and your sweet being. To learn who you are, you need to know the beginnings that shaped your character. To get to where you are going, you need to know the mental place you are coming from. If you think as you always have, you take the same mind-set with you and nothing changes. Your 'bio' frees the clutter to change your condition.

As a seeker of happiness, you must literally see who you are. Mulling things over, seeking advice from others, turning to books, reciting affirmations won't do much good until you do so. No wonder the message of inspirational books read, the counsel of voices listened to are of passing help. How can they make a lasting difference when what lies beneath remains covered?

Don't go negative with yourself and believe you can achieve the same result simply by giving the matter some thought. Nor do I wish to hear you haven't the time for writing, or you are of different color or speak a different language. I want to know you dare do what needs be done to have your place in the sun. You could look into the mirror and cleverly say, "Here I am." But who is "I am"? Do you know?

Writing your 'bio' is a thoughtful heart-to-heart with your soul. As you write, *you see what you are thinking*, bringing to light the people and events that helped to form your present mind-set; even unfilled dreams, once promising, come to surface. You may be surprised by what you uncover!

Memories of hurtful, harmful things done you will likely come into view. Don't forget those you may have done to others. As painful as this might be, in not wanting to confront them, you may pretend not to see. Yet, like pruning faded blossoms from a rose bush to sweetly bloom again, write the hurts out of your mind and "grow" again —such a gift to grow and bloom again.

While studying your 'bio' there you are, you can see the flower, *see who you are*. Don't become like I had become and not see a blooming flower.

You may find listening to music while writing is a connection to help express your thoughts and feelings. I don't suggest music like that of cats in concert—choose something soothing, songs or orchestrations that stir your emotions.

You ask, "Will writing my 'bio' change my life?" Maybe, but I don't think so. Your 'bio' begins your transformation, the end objective is to:

Identify the role your negative impulses are playing to see the emotional needs they are meeting.

Before you can own the life you dream of, you need to know the source creating negative tendencies—how and why they began. The negative stuff of the past is no longer happening, yet remains with you and needs to be identified and dealt with.

Somewhere in my head the describing words for the cause of negative impulses was revealed in my epiphany, if only I could flesh them out.

Feeling especially tired, I decided to lie down (again). All the "excitement" was taking its toll on me. My cat jumped on the bed and decided to lie beside me. I lay there petting my cat and fell asleep.

After a nourishing breakfast the next morning, compliments of my daughter who came to check on me, I continued with my ponderings. Not sure where to start, just like my 'bio' I began at the beginning.

I set my concentration on why we hold onto negative culprits while we yearn for happiness, then ponder why we are discontent.

What creates the emotional barriers to our sweet being? When do they start? Why don't we recognize the harms being done? Is an intrinsic need lacking in our awareness? If so, what is it? And why is the road of life filled with potholes for some, while for others their journey is a smooth ride.

I thought of friends, conscientious and hard-working to make their dream happen, only to fall short; bewildered by their unfilled wish of comfort. I thought of those successful, each day a celebration of life. Why the difference? Is happiness and good fortune programmed into our genes at conception? Or, the heir of fertile circumstance and genes are simply units of protein?

I recalled the empty faces that filled the doctor's waiting room, weary faces credit-carding at the mall, unhappy faces behind clenched steering wheels and the anxious faces at the seminar in search of a better way to experience life. I realized their expression reflected my expression, or vice versa?

I thought of those with smiling faces, their words spreading happiness—too few. Why so few? Does happiness come through making others so?

Though it was now clear I embraced the culprits that entered my life, often I found myself pondering, "Where are the defining words to describe what I thought I understood in my altered state?" Like instinct or intuition, you can't explain how you know, you just know. And many times I tried to grasp them, only to have the words elude me. Certainly my soul had to know how difficult this was with my ordinary thinking.

In the meantime, as the healing weeks passed, I was growing stronger, my eighty-two pound presence now an imposing eighty-six. And before long the sleeping daffodils were awakening, their trumpet blossoms heralding an early spring.

Gratitude

It was another lovely day, sunny, not too warm, a gentle breeze made it perfect. It was a quiet, comforting moment in time. I happened to be outdoors breathing in the universe when, from out of nowhere, "they" came.

Like dancing butterflies, the fleeting, elusive words fluttered into my head and as I held them in the sanctuary of my mind tightly, yet gently, so as not to lose a single one, I could scarcely breathe until I caught each one on paper.

As though on automatic pilot I went to my desk and in shorthand wrote the "words" held in my head, hopeful that I hadn't lost a one. Upon transcribing the symbols into longhand, I set my concentration on the exact instruction and meaning to be sure I had it right. I added a few words to be easily understood, the substance of the insight is unchanged.

Take a sweet breath and listen . . .

"You abide with whispers of the past, breathing a shallow ether, overcome by mindless matters, captive in a spiritless life.

"Release your bondage.

"Open your consciousness to the essential love that illumines. Let soul's breath inspire you, nourish and guide you, its promise fulfill the seed of your desire. Come dwell in the energy of love with the flower of truth."

Astonished such inspired thought came out of my head, concepts expressly foreign to me, I remained very still while tears of gratitude rolled down my cheeks for the blessing of the insight given me and thought . . .

Hallelujah! At last! The "unspoken" has entered my conscious mind to reveal the source of emotional conflict and how to overcome. The words paint a picture of a singular flower abloom in the energy of love's truth. Simply marvelous!

Come! Let's begin the journey to fulfill our soul's need to experience happiness.

I'd like to be your guide along the way and share with you lessons I have learned.

For all things we see and hear, learn and read, influence who we become.

PART II

A Sweet Breath of Life

Whispers of the Past

The first step you take will take you back in time when you were very small, to a place not consciously remembered. Ready? Don't forget your purpose.

The moment you took your first earthly breath, cried your first tears and "let go," your journey through a new and different world of consciousness began. The moment your eyes first opened, every expression, image, shape, outline, color – every thing seen has been entered in the network of your mind, under the care of soul.

On this breathtaking magical day, your well-being and development was placed in the care of your parents. Your beginnings depended on their intellect and moral conscience, and the fundamentals taught to them. Their behavior and even the everyday emotional environment of your new surroundings made lasting impressions on your essential nature. The influence of their parental guidance established your foundation and outlined the path you would take on your journey through life.

As you grew older, soon others—relatives, teachers, clergymen, friends, acquaintances, came upon the scene to pass on the beliefs taught to them. Their example and persuasion helped to influence the structure of your life and played an important role in who you would become.

And since that heavenly day to the present moment, **all the teachings, experiences, and impressions you have ever had have been recorded in the network of your mind, stored in the "memory room" of soul—memories that tell your life story.**

Let's stay a moment with the yesterdays and call upon some whispers of the past.

Remember when your parents, or others, would say, "My! Such a good little child you are!" when you did as you were told? How happy you'd be because you had pleased them. You may have earned a big smile, a warm hug, a sweet reward. When you didn't obey, remember the dire consequence of being spanked, physically or verbally? And those awful feelings suffered through afterward? Oh, those terrible feelings of rejection and remorse! You were certain you had fallen from grace and would never be loved again. Not ever.

As you grew older and wiser, you knew when you listened to the advice of others and followed their persuasion, you gained acceptance. Compliance with their wishes helped to create a compatible environment and, even more, their approval made you feel special. You were well liked and this emotion made you feel very good.

Remember when your playmates came to your door to see if you could come out and play? Their request certainly made you feel wanted; acceptance from your peers was very important to your ego. Remember how a negative remark could put you in a state of depression for days, or how the teacher's praise about your good work would make your day? Your feelings of self-worth conformed to what others thought of you.

I'm recalling a time in the third grade. The teacher, Miss Obermiller, was tall and slim with dark hair pulled into a sleek bun at the nape of her neck, and black-as-midnight laser eyes that could melt a candle. Her fastidious manner, almost clinical appearance, makes this story more poignant.

Miss Obermiller controlled us with an iron hand and we obeyed without question. Two of her rules were: we were not permitted to speak, or to leave our desk, without permission.

On an ill-starred day, I needed to go to the bathroom very badly. I raised my hand, waving, trying to get her attention. Without glancing up from the papers on her desk she told me to lower my hand, she wasn't answering any questions. Panic gripped me! Bravely, I raised my hand. Again, I was ignored. And then it happened.

I wet my panties, my dress; the overflow running down my legs on to the floor! The humiliation I experienced from the stares of my peers, along with ensuing weeks of their taunts, would prove to be one of the worst "spankings" of my childhood memories. Though I should have followed my pressing instinct and left the classroom, fear ruled against good judgment and my pitiful condition was the unwanted consequence.

(When writing my 'bio', out of the blue, this incident came to mind. I reasoned my anxiety when in a large group was the "culprit" meeting an emotional need borne a long time ago.)

And there was the time when I was very small and several playmates invited me to their "very private" picnic. We each were to bring a goody to share among us. When my mother gave me her permission to attend, I squealed with great delight. Yet, even now, as I call upon my soul to replay the bittersweet memory, a terrible sadness fills my being as I see one playmate offer a banana to everyone but me, then whisper to my best friend who then whispers to me, "She said her mother told her not to play with you." (To this day, bananas are in the fruit bowl. Graphic proof we *can* change the way things were.)

A few months after the picnic, I was taken to the children's home. The one constant I, and the other children, could count on was control over us by the matrons and staff. The fear of not pleasing others became embedded in my mind. Often my relationships were of a submissive nature to please and be accepted rather than an interaction of trusted friendship and love. (This is a prime example how experiences of childhood can damage one's emotional well-being for a lifetime.)

Your return to childhood may bring fond memories of happier days gone by, a time of joy and laughter shared with loving parents who afforded you life's privileges without its responsibilities. And yet, life has become overwhelming; you can't quite get it together, unable to satisfy your unsatisfied needs. And often, your thoughts return to the carefree days of childhood hoping to recapture the ease and contentment you once knew.

Your stroll into the past may evoke grim remembrance of a time of unending duty and great responsibility with little time for frivolity. Now, you find it difficult to occasionally "let your hair down" and engage in light-hearted fun, and you feel uneasy in easy settings as a sense of guilt comes upon you.

As you reminisce, a single working parent may come into view—a parent so overwhelmed with duty and weary from the everyday concerns of providing that the omission of their attention to you was the sad consequence. As your whispers awaken sad emotions of melancholy and "not enough hugs", you feel you were shortchanged and want to cry a little.

Perhaps you dread opening the door and entering the room of the past. An empty room that holds no one there for you, no one concerned about the care of your life or to comfort you with love. Painful memories of neglect, attended to by fear that became the controller of your thoughts, the director of your life. Uncared for, befriended by fear, the force of will comes into play to satisfy your emotional hunger for love and approval. And a quiet desperation fills the void, still.

Your glimmerings into the past may bring to light kindly parents who, not having been taught, were unable to teach, and ignorance was your mentor. Unprepared, you go about working hard, not smart, and lacking the essentials you greet each new day emotionally wrestling with life's struggle, regretting your lot in life—certain that life is simply unfair.

Do your whispers echo harsh, belittling words from those you thought loved you? Haunting criticisms reminding you, "You don't know what you're doing, you don't do anything right!" Now, seldom satisfied, you wear yourself out to do things perfectly; to have your way, the right way. You find it hard to get along with others, unaware your know-it-all attitude is the culprit that had its beginning in the past.

Your childhood souvenirs may bring into view a time of restriction imposed by parents who, concerned you might get in harm's way, sheltered and protected you from the vicissitudes of life only to leave you inhibited, unprepared for life's experiences. Now hesitant, afraid of the risk, emotionally you are unable to open the door to opportunity, or love.

Perhaps your keepsakes hold remembrances of a competitive parent who, driven with desire for you to excel above all, directed your thinking and governed your life, unmindful of your wants or yearnings. As your thoughts return to yesterdays, you recall when motivation turned to resignation and the emotional stress of a controlled childhood helped to create who you've become, regretting "what might have been".

I'm certain there are some "whispers" I have missed; your 'bio' will bring the culprits to surface.

Are any of the "whispers" mentioned reminiscent of your childhood? If so, note the feelings you are now experiencing. *Your response identifies the role your negative impulse is playing— you see the emotional need it is meeting.*

This needed insight gives clear understanding to why you react, silently or openly, to certain situations or someone's remarks; why you believe you get small respect, feel uneasy, become angry, or any negative response.

Enter on your 'bio', *see* it. The deep-rooted memory will forever remain to mess with your emotions until you do. Like the teacher who would have you go to the blackboard and write ten times or more you would not do whatever you repeatedly did wrong. Somehow she knew this would help to resolve your difficulty. It worked.

The whispers tell the story of but a few, and with each whisper we can detect the silent yet powerful influence in control. While the foundation was being set, the structure was being formed, establishing your sense of worth, moral code and values, trust or distrust in your insight, belief or doubt in your abilities, the need for acceptance and approval from others for validation of your magnificent being.

Let's visit the past a moment more.

When you were a child you may have been taught to say your prayers and were told only good little girls and boys go to heaven after life here on earth to the place where God resides, who knows your every thought, need, and desire. Likely, your image of heaven was "somewhere out there" apart from you.

As you grew older, you may have read the Bible, missal, Koran, or other religious book, as your parents had before you. Most likely, you attended the church of their choice, learned the church doctrines and understood that should you not adhere to its precepts, non-conformance would lead to sinful ways and keep you from God. You may have been taught salvation lies outside yourself, through the intercession of those closer to Him.

However learned, the spiritual comprehension held (one of the loudest whispers) was one of fear and dire outcome should you stray from the righteous path mandated by others – many, many years ago.

Keep in mind the dogmas ordained and decreed as law by church councils long, long ago and passed on to us were predicated on fear because they knew no other way to hold the people under their control.

There were times in my childhood when I felt something wasn't right. What was it? I wasn't getting through to Him, wasn't receiving answers. Were the grown-ups in touch? Was He answering them? Why not me? Then, one day, I discovered most adults were like me.

Your return to the past reveals the perceptions and impressions you now hold of your relationship with yourself, parents, others, and the Creator, are governed by the intellectual, emotional, and spiritual experiences of childhood.

You have discovered life's journey has been charted by the teachings and beliefs of others. When misguided, you struggle within, a stranger to your soul—unsure what you are looking for, yet in search of happiness, while waiting for your reward "somewhere out there".

The silent influence of the "whispers" weaves control over your essential nature, dictating the behavioral patterns you unconsciously follow each morning you awaken until you turn out the light and go to sleep. Throughout each day the recorded memories turn on your emotional response, which in turn dictates your mind-set— the contemplations and aspirations you present to yourself and to others.

The fundamental beginnings helped mold the thought condition, the expression on your face this very moment. And when the foundation is shaky, you are held hostage from realizing the unlimited potential of your magnificent mind, captive from giving happiness to your magnificent being.

Whispers of the past, memories indelibly etched on your mind . . . your soul.

In Captivity

We all have memories of childhood; some are clear as a bell, many are blurred, a fragment of the whole, and some so vivid as though happening in the present moment.

Some memories are like priceless treasures, sustaining as a sweet breath of life. A few are meaningful, forever enhancing life, many seemingly inconsequential, perhaps thought forgotten. And one or two so painfully wretched, they are not allowed entry into the realm of conscious. But *good or bad, all memories are powerful.* They are so powerful they control the friendship with your being; their unseen presence reveals who you were—who you've become.

Let's look into the corners of the mind and visit the place of "memories". Let's take a closer look at those that create muddled thinking, uncertainty and confusion – the ever present "whispers" that mess with emotions and damage self-esteem.

It's time to search every nook and cranny to confront the culprits who have cleverly crept in and hold you captive. A time to play detective and investigate to learn why life isn't all you hoped for, dreamed of; time to examine the core of your beliefs to see why you may not believe you are as wonderful as you are—for **nothing is as necessary as being happy with who you are.**

Should you have the slightest inkling your life is in a muddle, learn why you think and behave as you do to find the underlying cause creating uncertainty, confusion, an unhappy you. Your assessment must be clear and honest; there cannot be a shred of doubt. You cannot be at cross-purpose with yourself. If you just sit and wonder, nothing will change.

To meet success, gather all the self-knowledge you can, whether it seems relevant or not. Once the culprits come to light, you are closer to creating the life you wish to experience. Once the trouble makers (negative emotional impulses) are identified, you have the insight to make the necessary changes needed.

The most difficult to recognize are those which took root before the age of five. It has been proven the first years set the pattern for learning and behavior. To help, whenever you find you are experiencing a strong reaction to something, take note of your emotional response to what is occurring in the moment.

When teachings command and constrain, when impressions crush the heart with empty feelings of rejection and neglect, when experiences leave dark images that even closed eyes cannot erase, the recorded memories erect powerful barriers that separate ego from the soul. Barriers such as guilt, fear, shame or unworthiness that batter the spirit and shatter dreams. Barriers you unconsciously deal with, despair over and nurture each moment of every day of your life.

The powerful barriers control your decisions, great or small, and choices made yesterday are today's memories. And if today's memories are bitter, most likely tomorrow's choices will prove to be the same. The unwanted emotional consequence can last a lifetime.

The choices you regret the most are the ones you didn't consider the consequence. Be mindful what you wish for.

You are your choices.

When you are presented with a choice, evaluate its worth. Does it meet your morals or principles? Do you sense your self-respect may be in jeopardy? This assumes you place great value on yourself. Do you know your value—the worth you hold of yourself? If not, most likely you will make poor choices—find out.

The great harm of misguided teachings is the stifling of intellectual promise. Troubled, unmotivated to explore and develop, free will now surrenders to the controlling condition and the potential lies dormant, without expression, and sadly, the passion to succeed in any endeavor is looked upon with indifference.

This crippling of the intellect not only promotes ignorance, fears of every imaginable kind appear and bring about confusion, contradiction, uncertainty. Now, fuzzy impressions, muddled perceptions settle in making one incapable of forming definitive concepts, causing all sorts of woe to befall one self and others.

The child-like state of confusion invites more self-imposed limitations to take control and undermine their magnificent being, jeopardizing a joyful relationship with their soul, touching the lives of those who care.

When teachings inspire, encourage, and foster love, yet, for whatever reason, one gets lost along the way and takes up arms with disobedience or addiction, attacking those who stand in the way of their downhill path, ego's will is its own undoing. Troubled, hostility takes control to leave the spirit broken.

Unfortunately, for those with inadequate teachings and direction, the missing guidelines and lack of emotional connection are painfully in control.

You may have little self-regard and, because you do, have small regard for others. You may want all privileges with no responsibility and can become ungrateful, argumentative, willful, or cruel in relationships. You may grow dissatisfied with life and find fault with everything, and as your suffering twists slowly in the mind, become a martyr to arouse feelings of guilt or pity from others. You may find yourself addicted to food or substance to quiet the need for love and approval and capture a moment of comfort – an emotional cripple, out of control.

What is control? Why is it so important? Essentially, **control is authority, strength, and power**. How do you acquire control? Through knowledge—yes, knowledge of all kinds—self, spiritual, earthly, scientific, intellectual, et cetera. You are acquiring knowledge now. This is good! And the passion to acquire knowledge and reason it out grants wisdom. And this is *very good*, for wisdom grants clear thinking and sound judgment, blessing you with sweet reason.

Knowledge is the backbone, stirs the imagination to think good ideas and create great things. It bestows confidence. And what does confidence give? Courage! Ah! wonderful, sweet courage to go for your dream and see it happen!

Knowledge nurtures self-esteem, necessary for achieving a sense of self and taking control of your life. Self-knowledge empowers you to clearly define your credo –absolutely essential to celebrate who you are, what you wish to accomplish on your splendid journey through life. And the more you know, the stronger the confidence, the higher your self-esteem, the greater your creativity, the more you *really* like who you are.

So, it is more accurate to say control is the accumulation of knowledge and the reward is authority, strength, and power. *Scientia est potentia!* (Knowledge is power.) Control is very important for when you are not in control, or when you are out of control, you are powerless. Like a ship with a broken rudder your course is aimless and erratic, adrift on the stormy sea of confusion, headed for the Port of Troubles.

Should you find yourself beside yourself, distressed for whatever reason, and should a moment of clarity light upon you and sense you are out of control, you can be certain a state of confusion and anxiety have taken hold.

If you find life is a chaotic condition where too many things go wrong or get in the way of living, you can be certain confusion is the negative constant playing with your emotions.

Confusion: out of control; the inability to distinguish between order and disorder; aimless action. The extreme of confusion: a troublesome life, a void.

To illustrate, perhaps the reality of your early beginnings was one of much activity where you learned to expect the unexpected. When, without rhyme or reason, each day was a surprise and six or more activities were happening. Today, you wear yourself and others out, too busy to hear what your thoughts are trying to convey; a captive of the emotional confusion of the past.

Ease up. **Fatigue creates confusion and disorder.** Relax with a sweet breath of life. You have all the time in the world to enjoy and make the most of life's journey. Yes, you do.

When self-confidence is lacking, differing teachings can create conflict leaving lasting impressions on the mind. Unable to trust your judgment, you puzzle over which concept to embrace and look elsewhere for confirmation while indecision entertains the confusion in your head.

Suppose your favorite high school teacher thought the philosophy of Immanuel Kant was the one to embrace. Upon attending college, you find Carl Jung's logic makes more sense. Yet you vacillate, reminding yourself that your teacher was the greatest and how could she have been wrong? Besides, weren't you okay with Kant's view? Hesitant to commit to either one, confusion holds you captive and questions your philosophical belief.

Perhaps you embraced the religious belief of your parents, then upon going out on your own found another spiritual doctrine more to your way of thinking. Now, feelings of doubt or betrayal hold you from daring to make a choice. Confused, you vacillate, unsure what you want to believe is what you should believe.

Think of the times you allow, even encourage, the views of others to decide your course of action, persuasions that can affect the outcome of your life. The quandary may be as inconsequential as what color outfit to wear to the ball game, or as decisive as considering a career change.

Your dependency had its beginnings in the past and has become a habit.

If you're unable to make a decision without consulting another, if you haven't the courage to state your convictions for fear they will meet disapproval, unconsciously, you doubt your reasoning ability, unable to clearly sort out your thinking or grasp what your thoughts are trying to convey.

Uncertain, believing your decision will be met with criticism from the family or ridicule by your peers, you search out others for the direction to take believing their answer is the right answer. And with their thoughts in your mind, confidently follow through with their thinking, now certain "your choice" is the right one. What's more, not only do you have their approval, you have someone to blame when the outcome is less than hoped for.

I'm sure you've heard others, or yourself, mutter, "I don't know." Unsure, afraid of stating the wrong answer, self-doubt, a step-child of confusion, awaits the "knowing" answer for this is what it has been conditioned to do. The voices heard today echo the whispers of the past.

And so, you muddle through life avoiding answers, escaping decisions, making poor choices, because you would rather be "right" than wrong. Because confusion is in control, you haven't the slightest notion you are confused. Consequently, you feed your mixed-up self with empty ego trips, protecting it with all your misguided might and you are in a whole lot of trouble with a big "T" for the rest of your life.

You might ask, "What is wrong with listening to others, benefiting from their knowledge and experience?

41

After all, they may be wiser than I." This may be true.

The significant point is: when reliance on others is your validation, how will you learn to rely on yourself? Acquire self-confidence? Know your true thoughts or convictions? Create your experiences? When dependence on others is your style, the opportunities to develop your potential may never return again.

As you look to others for answers, the one certainty you will surely come to know is who they are. But who are you? Do you know? When following their direction, who is experiencing the adventure of your goal? Are you not living through another's perception for the attainment of your desire? How will you know where your talent lies?

You must know nothing is more emotionally rewarding than reaching a goal you set for yourself.

To learn what you do best, ask yourself what makes you happy.

You think and do your best when you are happy.

If you say "yes" when you should say "no", you empower others to control your life. Your failing tells others who you are.

I once worked with a nice gentleman who couldn't say "no" to anyone. Yet, he went about doing what others, unreasonably, wanted of him. His accommodating way gave him the sense of acceptance and approval he needed to feel good about who he was. His uncontrollable need to say "yes" not only created disharmony with others at work, his family suffered as well. And with "more stories than a high-rise", his excuses quietly controlled others in that he seldom met his appointments on time, and his work almost never honored the promised completion date.

Often, to pacify his clients, he would accept meager payment for work done.

The less responsible you are, the more dependent you are. The less your self-control, the more others will control you. Whether your life's work or affairs of the heart, you can't play both ends and succeed. Sometimes, saying "no" is liberating—of benefit to all.

Conversely, when focus is centered on how others conduct themselves, unconsciously you may be trying to exert control over them. Your concentration on others may be so strong that you are forever questioning their actions, checking their progress at work or at play, distrusting their ability to perform as you believe they should perform.

The need to control others controls you, making it clear you aren't in control.

When you distrust the actions of others, don't respect their wishes, this is a "red light" signaling you to stop and ask, "Why don't I?" Were you brow-beaten, ordered what to think and do, abused in childhood? Your mind-set reflects who you were, and the loss of self-esteem has created small confidence in who you have become. You are transmitting the reflection of you to others.

You must take a good look at the harm the "whisper" has done—assess what you uncover. As with all culprits, **identify the negative impulse to see the emotional need it is meeting.** Decide to free your sweet being from the influence of the "abusive" culprit of the past and create a self-confident you. Run from those who make you feel bad – never go back and keep company with those who undermine you. Not ever.

When you are uncertain why you are doing what you are doing, not sure where you are going, not meaning what you say, you create separation. **As you treat yourself less, others will treat you less**, and you will puzzle why you attract superficial people into your fairy-tale life. You must like who you are before others can like who you are.

Perhaps, like me, you invested time and energy (and money) on inspirational books and seminars, even sought professional counsel, but nothing seemed to work. The words of wisdom lay on the surface; the stirring thoughts didn't sink in. The sensitive words, like hothouse plants, faded away in the uncontrolled environment. And the affirmations? Robotic recitations, soon forgotten. And there you were, back from where you started, puzzling why your efforts seem for naught, searching for that "something" missing from your life, hoping to find the "something more" to fill the emptiness within.

So, why is happiness so hard to achieve, even in day-by-day affairs? Like a yo-yo, one moment you're up, you've got the world on a string; the next you're down, wondering why happiness is so elusive. And why trouble over it? After all, you aren't that muddled, nor are you always unhappy. There are moments of joy, like a well-deserved raise or bonus, the Yuletide season, a box of chocolates. Besides, you manage to make the most of what you have, somehow.

Well, the difficulty arises from the control of the whispers of the past. You won't let go, your past belongs to YOU. So you remain, content with your discontent—or shall I say, discontent in your "contentment".

Fortunately, your being is quite capable of re-learning what it has learned, all the while preserving the past in safekeeping in the storeroom of the mind.

For example: take the multiple of 4 x 4. If you memorize 4 x 4 = 15, you believe this true and incorrectly apply it. Your inmost being accepts this as truth. When you learn the answer is wrong and through conscious involvement of writing (your eyes must see the correction), you correct the equation to 4 x 4 = 16, the consciousness of your inmost being will accept the correction and file away the mistaken thinking to the reject pile, stored in the memory room of your mind. By literally making the correction you erase the previous belief or learning held, thus changing your mental environment, your mind-set.

So it is as you identify the role your emotional impulses are playing and decide they are creating unwanted outcomes, a marvelous transition occurs. Your inmost being effects changes and now, intuitively, you apply your new truth. You are planting the seeds of change, reprogramming your thinking.

Once you trust this truth you are free, confident in the knowledge that while you are making necessary changes, the past still belongs to you.

Now that you have been rummaging through the past, poking into the cupboards of your mind, most likely you sense a difference taking place within. As you ponder (and write), you are cultivating a friendship with your inmost being. In response, the "anima" within is nurturing you. This is good, very good.

But we need pause. Emotional needs may require additional help, a special kind, to make necessary changes.

To help cast the cunning culprits forever into exile, a primary requisite is called for.

This *sine qua non* (requirement) provides the insight to help you resolve emotional confusion, the logic to intelligently execute your endeavor.

We are now approaching the realm of Essential—the place that nourishes and guides you, supplies the insight to create your happiness. The pause that refreshes. The inspiration with every sweet breath you take. Your true-blue best friend who just makes you feel good! That magical place to help you find your way—that tranquil place called Essential.

Come! We are on our way out of captivity!

PART III

A Place Called Essential

When you wish to drive somewhere you get into your car, put the key in the ignition switch, choose a gear, then press the accelerator pedal to set the car in motion. If you sit in the driver's seat staring at the car without making the connection, you won't go anywhere. It doesn't work.

When you wish to talk on the phone you lift the receiver or cell cover and press the connecting number to your party. If you listen for a voice without first making the connection, you'll be talking to yourself. (Sometimes, this works!)

When you are uncertain about the meaning of a word you refer to the dictionary, the point of reference. If you search through the newspaper for the word's meaning you might enlighten yourself with the news, but it's unlikely you will find the definition in the daily gazette. You have accessed the wrong reference.

Everything, yes everything, has its connecting place, a point of reference to carry out its purpose — even you, and me.

If you are dreaming your dreams but they aren't coming true, if you are talking to yourself but aren't getting answers, if you haven't found what you've been searching for, it is time to learn why not.

It's time to establish your connecting place so, instinctively, you turn to yourself, a time to identify your point of reference to access the source for the answers which you seek. I wish to boldly state this is how to make the happy difference in your sweet being, your life. This is "essential" for you to meet success—there is no other.

Let's begin.

Think quiet. Let go of what you're thinking, put your emotions to rest. In quiet, you are conscious of your soul's vibration, you are one with the presence in your mind. Take a sweet, deep breath and slowly let it go—feel it. No hurry, no worry, you do have all the time in the world. Again, take a slow, deep breath; savor the sweetness, the strength and comfort, soul's energy gives to you. Once more, take a slow, deep breath and access the source within: "I honor you, my soul, my sweet breath of life; you fill me with great joy."

Stay a moment; let the power of the connection work. Stay a moment in soul's embrace.

Breathe slowly, breathe deeply. It is impossible to be uptight when you do. And make the connection; ego's disconnect stills the soul.

Before we continue, did you follow through? I hope so – don't be lazy, don't deny yourself.

Seize this moment in time and space and make it happen. *Carpe Diem!*

I promise, when you take the time to consciously take sweet breaths each day, you will change and you will say, "I am a different me. I am a happy and wiser me."

Are you wondering, "What do sweet breaths have to do with who I am? Why must I take three breaths? Why not two, even one? And how will accessing my soul help make the difference in my life? I go to church, say prayers."

I'm not surprised by your questions, nor do you have to or "must do" anything. I want for you to experience how good you can feel, how sweet life can be.

First, let's understand the purpose of the Essential. Clear and simple, it is the oneness of ego and soul.

Ego: conscious thought, free will, earthly love - and **Soul: inmost thought, intuitive logic, inherent love**.

This is the realm of Essential. This is the partnership to help you to succeed in your purpose and experience happiness – your responsibility to your gift of life.

This is how it works.

When you consciously take deep breaths, awareness of the flow of energy centers you, directing attention to your thoughts and feelings. Your tribute sets in motion the interaction of ego and Soul—the Chairman of consultation, contemplation, introspection. You (ego) are accessing the intuitive logic of soul consciousness, the voice within, for the help you seek.

Whenever you are asked to try something new, the question you must ask is: "Does it work?" (Will it serve my purpose?) This is why this works.

As you take deep breaths, the "inspiration" calms while it energizes you. (This is good.) The interaction secures a sound relationship with ego and soul, conferring faith in your self. (A positive mind-set is essential.) With ego and soul in oneness you do your finest thinking, freeing you of emotional culprits that hold you captive, allowing you to make the most of yourself. (This is very good.) The realization you can access the voice within bestows confidence to take control of your life and make it better. The reality of this truth strengthens and comforts you. You accept yourself. You know who you are, where you are going. Excellent! "Yes, it works."

Repeating magic words like "I am wonderful, blah, blah, blah," isn't going to do it, for your soul already knows you don't really know who you are. You can recite, visualize, repeat affirmations, make resolutions, read all the books in the library, but if ego isn't interacting with soul, doesn't know how, perhaps believing soul is some mysterious entity, your circumstance will remain the same. As soon as the reason for the Essential permeates your being, it isn't necessary to repeat affirmations of how wonderful you are, you *know* this is absolutely true.

Still, doubt may cause you to ask, "If I define who I am in writing, why access my soul?"

Precisely, who is "soul"? Soul, also known as love's breath, is the Anima of life, the source. **Soul is vital spirit, prime mover, the seat of emotions of your inmost being**. Without the emotional intelligence of soul you would be like a robot without feeling or free will, absent of conscience, unable to commit to anything. Soul makes you human. Soul is your true-blue friend.

Soul is the inside voice of introspection. Introspection is a conversation with your soul. Whenever you feel the need for self-examination or guidance, this is where to come to talk things over. Here you analyze your capabilities and shortcomings to receive insight and clearly see where you are headed. When the input of soul is absent, ego's free will may take the wrong path in search of the happiness so desired.

When was the last time you embraced your soul? Yesterday? A month ago? Years? Never? Horrors!

I don't have "seven steps to success" or "eight rules for a happy life", but I can offer you the power of a sweet breath of life. My thoughtful purpose is to inspire you to be more than who you are and create the life you wish for. I take sweet breaths often to help guide me to help guide you. I'm aware this manner of uniting ego and soul may seem strange, only because this is new.

Had you been taught this way in childhood (and your parents, too) you wouldn't give it a second thought. Had you known to access your soul being and be best friends, you wouldn't be searching. Imagine how glorious life might be had you known *how* to interact with your inside voice when you were a child.

Interaction between ego and soul is a must. Make no mistake and dismiss this union. For every outside there is an inside. Like the relationship of nature and nurture, to disregard one is to diminish the other. Anything not cultivated will die.

If on occasion you "take a sweet breath" thinking this will magically change your life, know disappointment will follow your great expectation. Yes, it will.

You may have difficulty remembering to access your voice within. This is understandable, this is new and different. Don't become discouraged. I truly believe, often enough when at the children's home, the remembrance of my mother and me taking sweet, deep breaths was the inspiration I needed to comfort me, to motivate me.

(If you didn't receive comfort from someone when you were small or even when you grew bigger, seek the company of those who presence you find uplifting, brings you alive – most likely they are in harmony with their soul.)

Keep in mind **your emotions transmit your feelings.** In the next second, hour, day, you act out what is going on within. If you are entertaining dark thoughts or suffering with an addiction, or allowing anger to fester and eat away at you, turn to soul friend for courage to overcome the demons. Banish the culprits that sabotage you, your Essential being.

Place reminders where you are sure to spot them, until a "sweet breath" becomes instinctive, like breathing. Remind yourself you are uncovering the "essence" of you. Most likely, much of your reality is through others—family, friends, acquaintances, teachers, bosses, co-workers, customers, your pets and, of course, television, Internet, electronic gadgets, iPads and like instruments.

I must confess there were times early on I'd forget. A day or so might go by before I realized how good I had felt. Talking to my soul I learned to like me. I became more confident, my self-perception was undergoing a change allowing me to interact with others in a more positive way. This was so good, for in the past, unsure, afraid to take the first step, my meekness had often been mistaken for disinterest or aloofness. Most of all, I experienced feelings of contentment. Ah! wonderful, sweet contentment!

If you have lost your zest for living, if life has become jaded and you'd like so much to feel good again, take sweet, deep breaths – again and again. If nothing else, the increase of oxygen will lift you up. (Pun intended.)

Each time you make the connection, breath by breath, you are silencing the emotional culprits separating ego and soul. When ego and soul become one "free will will free you to release your bondage", enabling you to clearly define your credo for living, and joyously celebrate life—your true legacy as a child of the universe.

To help nurture the oneness of ego and soul, the opportunities for taking a sweet breath are endless: while waiting at the stop light, visiting the dentist's office or beauty salon, shopping at the mall, taking a walk or lying on the sofa, ad infinitum. Pause and take a "breather". Breathe deeply—think about what you are grateful for. Thoughtfully say something like, *"Your blessings energize my being and I am gratified."*

These momentary reminders do leave everlasting impressions on your mind, making the positive difference in how you feel and interact with others. It takes only a moment to fill idle moments of the day with your sweet being. Truly, what can be more important?

In the morning, while I'm awakening and my senses still in sleep mode, the taking of sweet breaths is the inspiration that creates a happy me. The change in my attitude fills me with desire to create a wonderful day. And with all the crazy happenings in the world and climate change upon us, sometimes when I get out of bed, I'll say, "Good morning, world! I'm so glad you are here!"

You create your habits and failure, like success, becomes a habit, for this is what you have become accustomed to. Feeling sad is a habit, almost comforting for some. If this helps to define you, change it, everything needs a start. And like the caterpillar transforms into a butterfly and experiences happiness, you, too, can fulfill your soul's need for happiness.

When you awaken, stay a moment longer and take a sweet breath or two, or more. This moment in time is the most rewarding. Not yet fully awake, without distraction or interruption, you are in the ideal mental place to embrace your soul for a pleasantly brief "conference" on the higher level.

Your conversation may center on your dreams to reveal a lot about your emotions, or how you plan to create a magical day. This awakening starts your day with a positive outlook, opening your consciousness to see the infinite opportunities that await—golden opportunities you might otherwise miss and may never return again. This centering reminds you to return to yourself throughout the day, and this is very good.

If something is puzzling you, when you go to bed tell your soul. While you are sleeping, soul's intuitive logic can be working on the solution. Soon, or perhaps the very next morning, the answer to help resolve your dilemma will enter your consciousness. Don't forget to express gratitude and joy for the end of a perfect day. Your soul loves a thoughtful ego.

When I am still, I call upon my soul and say, "Tell me what you see that I should know." Since many of my dilemmas are resolved while I sleep (and often wake me up), I decided it merited a tribute:

"Introspective conversations are a great delight, transmitting answers through the night."

After visiting with your inside voice, whether for a

moment or longer, you should experience a feeling of calm, yet revitalized and in good spirits. If not, you aren't concentrating, aren't connecting. If your thoughts wander, learn to discipline yourself or the moments will leave no impression, have little meaning. Those who see their dreams come true have learned introspective conversations helped to make it happen.

Interaction with soul can't be a sometime thing. You must be dedicated. Repetition is effective, and practice makes perfect, demonstrating clear thinking, and clear thinking is power! Can it get any better?

Once ego and soul become best friends, your attitude undergoes a change—your outlook is rosier, brighter. The energy once expended on self-doubt now inspires confidence, and the need to look to others for confirmation has lost its charm.

Should you fall along the way, a sinking feeling has you vowing never again let this happen. You are becoming wiser, more loving, simply by taking sweet, deep breaths—anytime, anywhere. For free! You also discover the "inspiration" not only inspires you to think happy, to do better and see the good, it is contagious.

Your positive energy is an inspiration to others.

What soul wants is for ego to be in touch, the very best of friends. As you reach higher levels and see how magnificent you are, all you are capable of achieving, you will be ever so grateful ego and soul became best friends.

You have entered the realm of Essential and have the formula for the way out of captivity—the oneness of ego and soul. No one can take this from you — yours every moment of each day, yours to have but forever.

Soul is patiently waiting for your return, for you are the caretaker of your soul.

Being open-minded to a new way of thinking isn't easy, and embracing a different view does necessitate a decision. What will be gained, how much lost, is crucial to every decision, but you do need to decide. At this moment, the choice is yours to make the difference in your life. Keep in mind, the choices you make help define who you are; the life you will live. Remember, **you are your choices**.

You have several choices. You can choose to forever remain in captivity, shackled to the culprits of the whispers of the past, or to let ego's free will free you. You can console yourself with the thought your parents and grandparents, or society are responsible for your destiny, and put it to rest. You can let five years roll by while you ponder why life isn't what you hoped for, dreamed of. You can wait for a miracle to come along, hoping your humdrum life will go away. But it won't go away. You make the decision. YOU decide.

Why not seize this moment in time and space to embrace the sweetest friendship of your life? You know life is precious and the moments must count. Decide to be best friends with soul. You know how to make this happen. Just "do it".

For some, the following may be the "magic potion" they unconsciously search for to free the shackles of emotional distress, one thing more before closing the door on the way out of captivity—time to take your medicine, the wonder drug called Forgiveness, also known as "letting go". The label on the bottomless brown bottle reads:

Forgiveness – for the release of guilt or blame
                removal of doubt and distrust
                remedy for pain or sorrow
Symptoms – confusion, remorse, resentment
                repressed anger, hate, vengeance
                desire to emotionally punish oneself

If the past has left you broken or disillusioned, can you cherish yourself when you are filled with remorse? Can you fully experience joy if you are angry? If you are consumed with doubt and distrust, can you embrace friendship and love? You must forgive and let go of negative whispers of the past for your release to be realized. You cannot access higher thought or dwell on the higher plane with an unforgiving past in the presence. Your presence is each new moment of life.

Forgiveness is the remedy, forgiveness purges ill will.

Forgiving the misguided truths you've been taught and those you've acquired, forgiving the harms done and those you have done to others, in letting go of them you master them. No longer room for anger, hate or remorse. You change because you have forgiven. This is the wonder of the wonder drug called Forgiveness.

The following tells the distress suffered when forgiveness is denied, whether for a moment or a lifetime— a note written to me by my then nine year old granddaughter, Emily, after a misunderstanding.

"Accidental mistakes are made daily, mostly when hearts don't realize it. Love can only fix ones that were meant to be fixed. You make a mess, but are too sad to resume. When you hurt a loved one's feelings, you truly hurt your own. You can't stand the pain-tingling all around. You meant to say it this way, but instead said it wrong. You want forgiveness by the world.

You want to dive in and say you're sorry, but something pulls you back. So, finally, you blurt it out after tears and sobby cheeks. The hardship the person faces raises higher than your own. Take the time to realize how close we are, because then we'll be happy and enjoy fun."

So, you see, **forgiveness is letting go to let happiness enter**. When you forgive you let soul in to free the bondage of a moment or, perhaps even years. Now is the perfect time to forgive, the perfect time to let free will free you.

Think quiet. Let go of what you are thinking, put your emotions to rest. In quiet you are conscious of your soul's vibration. In quiet, you are one with the presence in your mind. Take a sweet, deep breath and slowly, let it go. Again and make the connection, "I honor you, my soul, my breath of life, you give me great joy. I am forgiving of those who placed me in bondage. I let go of thoughts that hold me in captivity. I forgive and release blame. I forgive and release the pain and sorrow of the past. Your love and my free will let me let go. I am free. My heart rejoices!"

Stay. Let this truth permeate your consciousness. Stay a moment in soul's embrace. Savor the sweetness, strength and comfort soul love gives to you.

This may be the most defining conversation of your lifetime. You will be ever so grateful you took a moment to visit with your friend. Don't let regret settle in—just do it.

~~ essentials ~~

Have you begun your 'bio'? I hope so.

Here are a few thoughts to examine and consider.

Let's begin. **To begin is to think.**

"Am I in harmony with my being, comfortable in my company? Am I content, pleased with the condition of my life?" If the answer is "no", try to identify the source and learn why you choose to remain. Perhaps you are afraid to face what you don't want to see; confront the culprits that muddle you.

Don't just read the words, spell out your feelings. *See what you are thinking.*

Ask: "Am I responsible or do I look to others to think for me and supply my needs, as in childhood? Am I loving? Motivated? Vital? Or am I usually tired, drawing energy from others? Am I working toward something I'm not sure I want? *Do I know what I want?"*

"What am I looking for? Acceptance? Respect?" When you don't respect yourself, you cannot expect respect from others. If you hang around with others who don't exhibit self-esteem, you soon will have small faith in yourself and your abilities, unlikely to ever experience happiness.

"Do I please others because I want something in return, or do I please because making others happy makes me happy? What gives me pleasure? Comfort?"

Do you only meet strangers? Perhaps, they are a mirror of you. **When you aren't sure of yourself—who you are—you are divided.** Subconsciously, you don't place trust in yourself. Will others have faith in you?

If you haven't done so yet, now is a good time to commit to paper the teachings and experiences that formed your beliefs to identify the underlying cause of negative emotional impulses that create trouble — sometimes, big trouble.

You want to see your inmost nature to learn where your emotions are taking you. Don't allow the past to muddle up the present and bury your future.

Self-knowledge is the vital link to creating joy in life, and for giving joy to others – one of man's higher accomplishments. This examination is sweet satisfaction to soul, of great benefit to ego, an emotional delight. Very interesting, certainly enlightening!

If you think you haven't the time for introspection, would rather continue living "blind," or if the motivation is lacking to spell out who you are, at least give your magnificent being some thought. Or, if you decide you simply can't take the time—you're right, you won't, and life will go on without you.

What you envision you bring to happen.

Whenever you make a change in your thinking, like tossing out negative impulses rooted in the past, spell out the new behavior. Literally, you are making the necessary change needed. This is not impossible.

If you sincerely wish to improve your condition, the design of your life, it is essential to know where your thoughts lie, what they are trying to convey. No need to suffer with misgivings or retain a shrink—write! Whether it is a daily to-do list, a little love note, a diary, or more importantly, your 'bio' — write to *see what you are thinking*.

Keep in mind there are no short-cuts. Like a little one learning to walk, small steps taken give confidence to explore new horizons, very interesting possibilities.

*   *   *

Friendship with soul is the Essential necessary to transform thinking and fulfill soul's need to experience happiness.

Now is a good time to visit soul.

Pay tribute, "I honor you my soul, my sweet breath of life, you fill me with great joy."

Stay a moment, savor the sweetness, the strength and comfort soul gives to you. Stay a moment more in soul's embrace.

. . . And Its Center

If you live to be 80 years old you will breathe 500 million times. If you consciously take two deep breaths a day, only 58,400 breaths or 1/100 of 1 percent of your lifetime will be in awareness of you.

Now is a good time to have some deep breaths in the company of your soul being. Take a deep breath, once more, and again. Be your friend's best friend. It only takes a moment, why not now? I'll wait for you.

* * *

What is your center? Your center is the power that energizes every thought, the force that generates the pulse of your vibration, the source of electro-magnetic energy from which life stems. *When you enter your center, you connect to the energy of soul consciousness to be one with the most magnificent being on earth.*

Please read the last sentence again. Ego has right of entry, permission to call upon and visit with the source within. Whether the free will of ego chooses to do so is dependent on ego's mind-set.

Whenever there is a need to resolve a dilemma and do some contemplating or to have an introspective conversation, like needing help to let go of negative influences of the past, "enter your center". Just like the conscious taking of sweet breaths inspires the connection of ego and soul to restore balance and harmony, the center of Essential ascends thinking.

When you are in balance (composed and collected) and harmony (of one mind) and your focus is centered within, it is then you receive the insight of soul to experience perfect thought condition. To experience perfect thought condition is a real "high". Here is truth without qualification or defect, pure and excellent; the source and power, the moving force and principle, the sum total of all things in time and space.

In perfect thought condition you know this is the place to receive the answers you seek – how unlikely it is to arrive at incorrect solutions, wrong conclusions. Here, there is no room for fears and imaginings to muddle-up thinking with senseless, mindless matters. There are no pretenses, no need to make an impression. There aren't any threats. *You see yourself as you are, the condition of your life, to change or glorify it.* Here, in the energy of soul's love, with the condition of truth, is the intuitive logic of the higher intellect of soul.

Intuitive logic is indwelling, individual with every being. Whether you are an Einstein searching for an elusive mathematical equation, a lyricist trying to find sweet expression for a love song, or an architect pondering over a design detail, higher intellect will unerringly compute ego's knowledge to help create the definitive answers for your specific need, or the direction perfect for you. When you access the intuitive logic of soul, the consultation will help supply the answers you seek.

I must tell you, some of my most fulfilling moments are when I am in perfect thought condition. Here I resolve my dilemma, create above ordinary thinking—at optimum, my mind surpasses itself. When you excel or better yourself, you validate your being; no longer the need to prove yourself. There is nothing like this experience, the intoxicating feeling of knowing you absolutely got it right! You have touched the presence within to be the best you can be.

My worst moments are when I am unable to experience perfect thought condition. Sometimes this happens. This is my clue I am out of sync in some way. Am I thinking quiet? Put my emotions to rest? Am I centered? Composed? This is a paradox, for perfect thought condition not only bestows enlightenment, it restores balance and harmony. One thing for certain, one cannot force perfect thought condition.

If you are in hopeless despair, suffering from ill health or poverty, or a broken heart, enter your center and in perfect thought condition have a conversation with the intuitive logic of soul. Will this suddenly transform your life into wellness, riches or happiness? No, I am not professing magical happenings. I am affirming "centering" gives advantage to think clearly.

I realize when you are down and out looking into a needy bank account, or suffering a lonely heart, it's difficult to comprehend how this can be the answer to your need. One thing I know for sure is accessing your center helps free negative thought to dispel concern and fear. I do promise that "centering" transmits healing throughout your being to ease your mind, rejuvenate your health, and nourish you with love. I do know the interaction with soul does help to make your heart and bank account full. The more often you enter your center, the sooner the magic happens.

When you enter your center, *let go of happiness lost.* Why try to recapture the heartache of "what might have been"? To dwell on past miseries won't change a thing, or even bring them back. Isn't that wonderful? These useless keepsakes only reinforce remorse and hold you captive, hold you to the least you can be. You must know these worthless thoughts are very expensive comforts.

I am reminded of a conversation with a co-worker some years ago. On occasion, his wife would meet him for lunch and a few times I was invited to join them. They were a lovely couple. One day he asked to speak to me, in private.

He confided though he was reasonably happy in his marriage and his wife pleased him most of the time, something was missing. He couldn't figure out exactly what it was, but his discontent was making him nervous, almost ill at times. He asked my advice. This was before I knew what I now know, a time when if anyone needed help it would have been me.

I don't know what caused me to ask, "What do you think about, where are your thoughts?" He stared at me, dumfounded, and then said, "That's it! I can't get her out of my mind! She was my first love, was all to me, and then, one day, she left. Bingo! She was gone." I said something like, "I'm sorry, but you must know dwelling in the past is like cheating on yourself, your wife and marriage. You must let go of the past."

Let go of happiness lost! Take a dose of forgiveness and let go! As you free your being, you can create the life you wish for. Think up! Think elevating thought, think truth and feel love. That bears repeating: think truth and feel love.

* * *

Because knowledge is essential to the success of any endeavor, I have gathered some bits of information relative to the chemistry of our being, along with some visionary thoughts about the workings of the mind. Knowing how your magnificent being works will help you enter your center without trepidation. Don't forget, knowledge is power—very big power.

Your being, basically composed of 99 percent carbon, nitrogen, and oxygen, is the balanced mix of elements and substances formulated from universal energy that embody your physical expression.

The electrical current flowing through your being is a stream of moving electrons producing energy; the energy that gives life and creates your distinct electro-magnetic field. The electrical current flows from the higher potential to the lower potential; i.e., the current flows from the proton (positive) to the electron (negative). The proton maintains its position in a stable manner and supplies energy for the circling electron to draw on.

One can't help comparing this universal law of nature to one's being. The positive being (proton) needs to create to have fulfillment. The negative being (electron) needs the creativity of others to experience pseudo-fulfillment. It does appear that mankind is the reflection of nature's natural law.

The electrolytes composed of acids, bases, and salts are liquid conductors that pulsate the electrical current of energy throughout your entire being every moment of the day, every day of your life, whether you are still, moving about, or asleep dreaming your dreams—ever constant, never ceasing, and seldom acknowledged or thought about. Just like your soul, true-blue, always there for you, to comfort and guide you.

When you are deep in thought, the electrolytes carry a strong current of energy to your contemplation. So it is when the focus is directed to your physical being. In an instant, perfect energy draws together your mental activity (mind), physical being (body) and higher intellect (soul). Here in the energy of your distinct electro-magnetic field is the vibration that is uniquely you.

An athlete whose concentration is set upon the game utilizes his electrical current of energy at optimum strength and harmony. For example, the tennis player: his mind swiftly computes the offense or defense he needs in his strategy to best his opponent. His eyes hold the suspended ball in his vision like a laser light. His body moves with speed and strength in less than an instant. His state of emotional tension electrifies his entire magnetic field, the electrical impulses pulsating perfect energy throughout his entire being.

Perhaps this is why games of sport are so well received and loved all over the world. The spark of life the players generate affects our magnetic field and "charges our batteries". The 100 trillion cells in our being react to the electricity in the air and are energized; the energy excites us.

Your being is inseparable. Your body and soul are one. They work and play together as one entity. If you are inclined to think sickness and disease, your body will exhibit fatigue and may even become ill, an (unwanted) response of negative thinking. When thoughts are inspired, your being mirrors the positive energy of positive thought.

Your being cannot contradict itself because the energy passing through your mind is the same energy passing through your body. The presence in your mind—soul—is the presence of your entire being, your every cell, everything within. Because your being is one entity, of itself is in harmony or disharmony.

Your neurons listen to every word, feel every emotion and expression on your face. Whatever you have thought, whatever you are now thinking, they send the data to the great storehouse of your mind, in the care of soul, to call upon at any given moment.

When a happy event occurs, notice how the positive condition brings a positive response to your entire being. Your pulse quickens, eyes sparkle and lips form a big smile; your countenance lights up, reflecting joy. You reach out to others to share happy feelings. You radiate good vibrations, drawing others into your positive electro-magnetic field.

When you are upset or angry and have spoken unkindly to another or, without a word spoken, thought unkind thoughts, the negative thought transmits negative impulses throughout your being. Your face becomes drawn, lips purse, the sparkle in your eyes disappear. You feel tired and agitated, are fretful, and sense nervousness within. Your being, in response to the negative mind-set, is evidencing the disharmony. This is not good! Don't allow this mind-set to help define who you are.

At the moment of conception, your being gets started with the inherited characteristics of the 16,000 genes the cells carry. Presently, science has classified 6,500, and 3,200 have been matched to specific chromosomal locations. DNA (deoxyribonucleic acid) is the essential component of all living matter in the chromosomes of the cell nucleus and contains the genetic code that transmits your hereditary pattern.

A genome is the total mass of genetic instruction and consists of strings of DNA nucleotides, the biological equivalent of "letters". The instructions on how to build a body are contained in the order of the nucleotide "letters" on the strings. There are 3 billion nucleotides in the genome. The stretches of hundreds or thousands of nucleotides are copied inside cells and direct them to produce specific proteins, the building-blocks of organisms. The stretches are called genes.

The genes within the cells have a memory bank to help with the learning experiences and happenings in life. Of this itself, cells have intelligence and instinct. When you use the inherent capabilities of the cells, not only do you benefit from the memory bank of the genes passed on to you, you add to their intelligence and strengthen future cell development.

If your inclination leans toward music and seems a natural to you, know your cells are prompting you to access the inherited knowledge of your genes, passed on from many genes ago. If you nurture the seed of your desire and pursue a melodic career, your musical knowledge will be entered and stored in the memory bank of your genes, which may be passed on to your children and your children's children—forever, without end.

When you pose questions such as how and why, you give your being the opportunity to increase your ability to think clearly and logically. Whether you are helping a child with their homework or working a crossword puzzle, you are stimulating your cells and neurons to develop and grow. You can be sure, your cells are delighted to show-off their (your) unlimited possibilities when invited to do so.

* * *

Let's turn our attention to the magnificent mind. Let's see how it might work. We can imagine the neurons in charge of different areas of the mind are "little men" pressing buttons (electrical impulses) to enter or access data, or store data.

The billions of neurons in your brain are endlessly communicating and interacting with one another. They never stop. They have set up an elaborate transmitting center to keep body and soul together. This unparalleled system is called the mind and consists of many components. Our interest is in the interaction of the conscious mind of ego and the intuitive logic of soul consciousness.

Everything conscious mind of ego sees and hears, learns and reads, is transmitted to soul consciousness. Soul's response becomes our emotions, our feelings, and can be evidenced instantly or delayed, set aside. This "everything" (memories of past teachings or experiences, or everyday happenings) is placed in safekeeping with the caretaker of the mind's storehouse, in the realm of soul.

When the conscious mind chooses to accept information, whether true or false, it directs the billions of helpers to file the data in the proper place. If conscious mind accepts that 2 x 2 = 3, the false truth is placed in safekeeping in the active file of soul consciousness. When conscious ego decides it no longer wants to accept what was once held as truth, soul conscious tells the "little men" to transfer the data to the reject file. But is never erased. Such as: reprogramming your mind-set.

When conscious mind is uncertain, soul consciousness directs the helpers (little men) to place the uncertain data in the pending basket for future consideration. In the meantime, the helpers search for and access any data that may be helpful to conscious mind in arriving at a decision. (Like when you ponder over which choice to make or direction to take.)

When soul consciousness sees conscious mind faltering, in an instant comes to the aid of conscious and supplies the urgent data needed. (This is your instinct.)

When conscious mind is in need of guidance or information, the consciousness of soul (intuitive logic) directs the helpers to access the relevant data. Sometimes, while the helpers search through volumes of files, the information cannot be supplied at once. When this happens and the free will of ego becomes impatient and rushes into unwise decisions or looks elsewhere for answers, the neurons transmit confusion to conscious mind.

If data has never been entered, it cannot be accessed.

When conscious mind has a new learning experience, the "little men" press the button to be entered into the active file.

When the mind is young, the teachings of others supply conscious mind with data. The consciousness of soul sees that the data is placed in the active file.

As the young mind matures and conscious mind develops, earlier teachings may create conflict. When conscious mind decides it no longer wishes to accept previous teachings, it can do so if no doubt remains. The unwanted data is placed in the reject file. If conscious mind isn't sure and the conflict isn't resolved, it is stored in the files of soul consciousness under "doubt and fear". This is why some find it easy to change their thinking and why others have difficulty.

Because our magnificent mind never stops thinking, sometimes stored data unconsciously comes to surface. Anytime negative thoughts come through, demand they leave! Reject the negative data at once! Let free will free you to reprogram your thinking and experience happy outcomes.

When conscious mind (ego) decides the purpose of taking sweet breaths makes sense, soul consciousness quietly, joyfully, assigns this truth to the active file.

More confident now with this knowledge of your being, ego can access soul without trepidation.

When you enter your center, this is place you come to contemplate on the higher level for help in your purpose, for guidance to help resolve your conundrum, for inspiration. Here is where the acquired knowledge of ego and the intuitive logic of soul get together to pave the way for your memorable journey through life. Here lies the answer, the direction for you. Here lies a sweeter, happier life. The realization is sweet; the condition, heavenly!

~~ essentials ~~

Take a sweet, deep breath of life, then another, and again. Breathe slowly, breathe deeply. Feels good, no? Yes!

Are your thoughts in a stew? Unless you let them go, they'll be there when you get back. Let them go! Put your emotions to rest, lay them on the pillow and let them rest. What is your being conveying? What are you sensing? Is it tired? Weary? Breathe deeply; breathe out your fatigue and fears; feel balance and harmony throughout your being. As you grow peaceful, perfect energy fills your senses.

Pay tribute, access your soul, ever there to strengthen you, comfort you with love. You are centered now; everything is prepared for you to think clearly. You are in command.

What will you do with all this power? You certainly don't want to think about the mundane happenings of the day, or the "what ifs" and "what might have beens". You are in control, without fear and limitation. This is the perfect time to see who you are, the path you have taken— to change or to glorify it.

Is what you see wonderful? I hope so. If not, why not? What are your aspirations, what do you wish to attain? What is important to you? Are you content with the life you are creating?

What will satisfy your hunger for happiness? Do you know? If not, find out.

If something is troubling you or seems missing from your life, enter your center and talk it over with soul. Whether you receive enlightenment now or at another time, in defining the wants and needs to create your happiness, you are gaining clearer insight into what you are in search of.

You have reached a higher level just by entering your center and having an introspective conversation with the presence in your mind. And this, in itself, is restful, reassuring, and good—very good.

Take a sweet, deep breath, and again. Stay a moment – let the connection work its power. Stay a moment more in soul's embrace, rest in comfort with soul love.

* * *

Now, with better understanding of why you have become who you are, the role emotions play, the knowledge of ego-soul connection and how your being works, let's journey on to see how thoughts entertained and attitude can create barriers to your purpose, the happiness you seek.

PART IV

A Sweet Breath of Life

Mindless Matters

Strengthened by the friendship of ego and soul, and the practical knowledge gathered, you are empowered, able to deal with the more stubborn of emotional demons that can possess you. (You can do this, you *can* be happy.) Let's examine these shady characters and cast them into exile—forevermore.

* * *

"Yet, you remain, overcome by mindless matters."

Of all the culprits most troublesome, can do much harm and help create wrong thinking to feed ego's distress, it would have to be "mindless mind-talk".

The definition of mind-talk is not in the dictionary. I believe it should be. Do you know what mind-talk is? It's what you are thinking, thoughts you are mulling over and over again and paying attention to; your very own private conversation, yours alone. If you are operating in the energy of soul love, I'm certain you are having wonderful, inspired conversations. If not, pay attention, this is for you.

When ego's mind-set is focused on mindless matters, the self-imposed barrier gives life to mindless mind-talk. The senseless chatter dwells on remembrances of the unhappy happenings of yesterday, the way things were, what might have been, or everyday matters of small consequence and evidence the emotional unrest within.

Emotions such as: anger, anxiety, depression; confusion, fear, suspicion, et cetera.

The disturbed thought condition of "what ifs and what might have been" repeat the sorrowful story of things past and present, the remorse of wrong choices and poor judgments made. The endless dirge smothers your being and holds you captive from creating and responding to new experiences. Rutted in the same groove, the dismal refrain spinning around your brain allows no room for inspired thought to dare think of entering. And yet, here you stay, listening; sitting in the rocking chair, going nowhere – restless in a humdrum life.

When mind-talk entertains thoughts of loss and regret, the discordant message is transmitted to every cell in your being. Your cells have ears and listen; their response to your truth becomes your energy. This feeble energy is visible on your face, heard in your voice, sensed in your attitude revealing your true nature, attracting those of like-nature into your world.

You must know you attract who you are.

I imagine you have experienced talking to someone who seldom had any good thing to say about anything or anyone, one who chose to air their mindless chatter until you could barely bear to hear one more word.

I once worked with a girl who had a "synthetic smile" for everyone, yet her empty chatter revealed her preoccupation with mindless matters, dampening the spirits of those whom she came in contact, they felt uneasy in her presence, her mutterings echoed her "whispers of the past". Eventually she was let go due to her criticisms of fellow employees' job performance.

Your attitude always conveys your mind-set.

One's aura radiates the truth its energy transmits. Every gloomy, negative thought entertained invites separation and will come back to haunt you. Clear to see why positive mind-talk is the recording to listen to. So, get wise, be smart and let go of mindless matters. Take sweet breaths—often. Be inspired. Reach higher! Be more.

Are you wondering why I am so familiar with mindless matters? When studying my 'bio' I could see the negatives and role they were playing to satisfy my emotional needs. I realized I was addicted to mindless mind-talk. What a heavy chain I wrapped around my being! The moment I am reminded of the place I once dwelled, like now, I shudder!

My childhood had programmed me very well and the senseless chatter continued throughout much of my adult life. I believe its seed took root during my "residency" at the children's home. Often criticized and belittled and, in my humble opinion, too often punished, I was forever in a state of emotional stress trying to please. Mindless chatter became my toxic friend. My mind-talk went something like this (very short version):

"Why do I feel so bad? What went wrong? I thought I had done it right. I really tried to please him (her, them, whomever) though I don't think I did. It's evident I didn't. I got little or no response, no approval. I was only tolerated. And after going out of my way, doing all I could, giving my all. Why was I shut out like a door mat? I feel like a door mat.

"Why does this keep happening? Maybe I need to be more interesting, more adaptable, more something. Let's replay the scene once again. I hope I did, or said, the right things. I feel all didn't go well. Why aren't I accepted? Why am I alone with this empty feeling, this heartache?"

And, on and on, on and on, I'd mutter to myself. My soul could only comfort me with the negative mumblings I transmitted to soul, thus nurturing my discontent.

How did I silence the chattering demon? When I was literally defining who I am, I could see my emotional turmoil was the result of decisions and choices based on my need to prove myself to others. Except for a few exceptions, my soul was a stranger to ego. (Or is that vice-versa?) Consequently, heartache was the empty reward, along with the stress of living with my wearisome chattering.

After learning the cause of my senseless prattle, from then on whenever I caught myself unconsciously muttering, I'd take a sweet, deep breath and erase. Soon, I parted company with the energy sapping demon.

Now, I am different. I please others because I want to, commit for the right reasons. If my presence doesn't please another, I shy away. I don't wish to give you the impression I dwell in "la-la-land" or live a hermit's life. Not so. Only to encourage you to break the spell you may be under and experience how good it feels to be free of the senseless chattering holding you captive from the contentment longed for. Once the spell is broken, clear thinking, coupled with a sweet countenance, will attract good into your life and you will wonder why you never thought of this before.

* * *

Some years ago, a friend whom I hadn't seen in ages came to visit as a guest in my home. Though I knew she had experienced some difficulties, I didn't know the extent of damage done to her.

During her stay, the conversation centered on the many illnesses and various operations she had endured. Each day began and ended with repetitions of the myriad of troubles to happen to her. The jobs that hadn't turned out right, accidents that were the very worst, the undesirable characters who came into her life only to treat her poorly. Like a discordant chord, her negative, distressing thought condition had me silently chanting a mournful tune.

After a few days of sympathetic listening, I tried explaining to my friend the futility of dwelling in the past; she needed to let go of the miseries to allow positive and good to enter her life. But my efforts were as successful as trying to unscramble scrambled eggs. Her mind was set. She wasn't ready to experience happiness. She liked living with the past in her future, or should I say, with her future in the past. One thing for certain, she wasn't in the present.

While waiting to board the plane to return home, her numbing chatter was still focused on mindless matters. One can easily see how those about her could surrender to mindless matters. Unless one is centered, this condition can be quite contagious.

We cannot enjoy what is placed before us when the leftovers are served again and again.

Talking about personal turmoil, silently or openly, won't make it go away; the despairing condition will only deepen. Nor should you fear expressing your views to help another and, perhaps, risking the relationship. Your pretense will worsen.

If there is little joy and laughter in your life and, too often, find yourself eavesdropping on mindless chatter, this is a good clue ego is out of touch with soul. Whether it is you, or another, who gives life to mindless matters, the senseless chatter is revealing the truth of your distressful condition.

If you are unhappy wherever you are, learn why you choose to dwell in darkness when there is so much living and loving to do; so much in life to celebrate.

Do you "invite" mindless matters into your life? Are you under their negative spell? When did they start? Recently? Or have they been your life-long companion?

What teachings or experiences have caused you to dwell with senseless emotional chattering? Was it chaotic, demeaning? Return to childhood and try to recall the very first "whispers" imprinted on your mind, the energy surrounding you. Do it. Until you change the worn out record, nothing will change.

Do you really want to look back to see life passed by while you were listening to the same tiresome refrain, missing the joy of living, the wonder of you? I think not.

Perhaps you are one who thinks, "I can't change. I am the way I am, my life is the way it is." Well, think again. You have the power to free yourself of the confounded culprit once *you decide you want a happier you, a better life.*

You can start now. Yes! Think a good thought, force yourself if you must—just do it. Greet each day, and others, with a happy face. And laugh. **Laughter chases every dark thought away, changes your outlook, transforms the relationship with yourself, attracting others to you**.

Let the sun shine on you, everyday.

I mustn't omit the second most troublesome culprit. It is silent; there is no recording to listen to for no entry is allowed into the mind. The culprit is stubbornness; won't listen, a "know it all" who won't take advice, yet insists on giving it. Its cohort is willfulness. At all cost, must be his or her way, or not at all.

The negative mind-set turns the emotions to stone.

If you have any inkling this may be you, who or what teachings have influenced you to create a closed mind-set? Identify the source holding you captive. Enter on your 'bio', see the demon isolating you in a dark place.

Don't be taken in by senseless culprits, whoever they may be. They come from the past and that's where they belong. A time to recognize the cause of discontent and unfulfilled dreams that tell your life story and play reruns of the same melancholic movie—the one titled *Empty Comfort*, with you, the star, acting out a poor script. What will the title of your new movie be? How about *Joy Revisited* or *My Soul and I* or even, *The Defining Moment?*

* * *

Sadly, on a larger scale, the producers of mindless matters have taken control en masse.

We are exposed to the degrading conversations on TV, the Internet, etc, that demean the magnificence of man. We see the barrage of bloody images, graphic celebrations of killing prowess that invade our sensibilities; the barely clothed women who showcase their "assets" and leave nothing for one's imagination; the explicit sexual scenes that deprive young minds of their childhood right to innocence.

We pause, but only for a moment, from the sleazy entertainment and puzzle why there is no moral ethic. The nanosecond of retrospection is soon replaced with more requests for the mindless producers (whom we have enshrined and made wealthy) to create more mindless matters for our mindless pleasure. And sad indeed to think, is this as high as we can go with our imagination? Is this the best we can be?

We have come to rely on others to think for us, we look to others to produce our experience, while our magnificent mind *lies captive in the cradle.*

And so, we go about as organic robots, automatically doing things in an automated life, not achieving the things we once set out to do, looking into an empty purse, living a spiritless life, where nothing is what it seems to be and everything is something else.

Not only do mindless matters create our ills and limitation, the inheritors are the children who listen, overcome by the endless, senseless chatter. *Our muddled thinking is teaching them to be the least they can be, as if to say, the least is the best. How shall we respect and love one another if we are the least we can be?*

One by one the things we say and do come back two by two.

Our "devotion" to mindless matters has lowered the academic standards to accommodate the undeveloped minds we are developing, while the sounds of music have become loud, discordant chords to fill the emptiness in our soul.

The street gangs and school bullies, their minds set on controlling rival gangs – destroying, stealing, molesting, killing, *killing!* – play the inherited, mindless record over and over again. Out of control, they inflict their pain onto others, believing this will "fix" their broken spirit. They perceive life as hell and, consequently, they live in hell.

Can you imagine the good these troubled children could bring to happen if the energy of their anger and hate turned to the perfect energy of love? Imagine how different their young lives might have been had only someone been there for them.

Oh! Where have all the parents gone? Their disregard numbs the child's soul; their absence defines who they are.

If we are to help the children we must first free our own bondage. As long as we send mixed signals, we can't hope for the children to make the most of themselves. Our conduct spells out who we are and when the "message" they receive reveals those whose examples they are to follow are without direction, who then can they emulate? Whose value shall they value?

We must learn who we are to restore self-esteem and create good thoughts and things, so our positive example will motivate and inspire the children to create good thoughts and things. Then they will know self-respect and, in turn, respect others. They will have the desire to think and create good, and experience the joy of being the best they can be. As will we.

Pause now and take some sweet, deep breaths.

Breathe slowly, breathe deeply. No need to hurry, you do have all the time in the world to have a quiet moment with you and your soul friend. Savor the sweetness, strength and comfort soul is giving to you. Feels good? Yes! Is good? Yes, very good.

Now, composed and collected, your mind-talk turns to happy-talk, nourishing your cells with good energy to think inspired thoughts. Your imagination is free to create wonderful things, your vision clear to make it happen. Your vibrant energy interacts happily with soulful others. You cherish your being, in balance and harmony with the universe. What a glorious feeling! Hallelujah! What a joyful time to be!

~~ essentials ~~

Are you getting involved with yourself, taking notes for your 'bio'? Remember, this is your life story.

When you spell out the "whispers" of yesterday's teachings and happenings, and digest what you have written, you can see the good stuff and the culprits that hold you in captivity. You can *see* where you are coming from. Isn't this enlightening? Yes! It's magic!

When writing your "bio", take note of emotional reactions to experiences that have left dark impressions on your mind, and in your heart. You want to feel now what you felt then to recapture the moment, helping you to identify the immoral or unethical cause of your distress, the unwanted feelings or behavior that now emotionally influence and help direct your life.

Make the decision to "throw out" the demon(s) and then let go! Yes, let go! Yes, it does require courage to bare yourself, even to your soul. But, **you must know, your soul already knew and had forgiven you**.

After an introspective conversation and, intuitively, you know what soul consciousness has stored away, you are closer to understanding why the path once taken didn't lead to all you hoped for, dreamed of.

Are you re-programming conscious mind to change your mind-set and experience the contentment of a happy life? You are responsible for negative feelings.

You have the power to make life better, whether health matters, profession or relationships. Yes, you do.

What is your purpose? Do you know? If you don't know or aren't sure, you will go from here to there, around in circles.

You do need to decide what you wish to accomplish, the path you will take to where you want to be.

If your purpose is to create a happier you, a better life, yet haven't the energy or desire to see why you think and behave as you do, know your old self goes with you and your present condition will decide. Yes, it will.

* * *

Are you familiar with this song?

"My sweet Lord, Oh, my Lord!
Really want to know you; really want to go with you,
Really want to show you, Lord
That it won't take long, My Lord
My Sweet Lord!"

George Harrison, The Beatles

Substituting the word Soul for Lord is a great reminder to visit with your inside voice.

This lyrical association stirs the emotions, brings you alive, inspiring you to interact with the soul of your sweet being, guiding you to succeed in your purpose, helping you to celebrate a happy life.

And this is very good. Yes, very good.

A Shallow Ether

Was stress your suffering partner again today? If so, I have the perfect solution to dissolve this wretched association. It takes but a moment. Take a sweet, deep breath, repeat, "No stress allowed here, absolutely none!" **Mutatis Mutandis!** *Necessary changes needed!* Aren't you breathing easier? Feeling more composed? Now, anytime the undesirable cohort makes an appearance, you know what to do. Soon, ego and soul will have formed the ideal partnership and stress, that shady character, will be gone from your life.

I wish I had made the merger when I was younger but, no room for regret, I have it now. No problems, just solutions.

* * *

"Yet, you remain apart from you, breathing a shallow ether . . ."

Stress is created from other emotional barriers; it is about the hardest to let go. Let's see who the culprits might be.

The most stubborn barrier to uproot is negative thinking. Easy to understand why since an attitude of doubt is ego's identity and with this cynical view, the positive attitude needed to change a tiresome life to a satisfying one is in jeopardy at the very start.

91

Negative thinking produces everything no one wants—doubt, distrust, grumbling, loneliness, illness, anger, suspicion, sarcasm, discontentment, restriction, uncertainty, failure, mulligrubs, etc., etc.

Pessimistic teachings may have taught you to feel comfort in a gloomy outlook, happy being unhappy.

Unfortunate experiences may have caused you to be defensive, lest others try to "cross the line" to do discredit and take control. Though others met aren't thinking such thoughts, the distrustful mind-set believing this is so retreats. The suffering consequence is a state of anxiety as life is viewed as a bed of quicksand. And with ego and soul in conflict, as strangers, self-doubt and limitation help to define the relationship with yourself, and how others perceive you.

When you dwell with negative thought you produce unwanted results, it's as simple as that. You expect the worst and worse is what you get. You expect to lose, so you don't take the risk. You can't quite get it together, nothing seems to work. The defeated outlook leaves you ineffectual to yourself and others.

I dated an attractive man who would show me a nice time—dinner, dancing, or the movies. Yet, I began to notice by evening's end I'd be feeling unsettled, almost down-hearted. After several dates, I was able to pin-point what was bothering me. During the course of the evening his skeptical view entered every conversation, he had something negative to say to just about everything. I determined a lack of trust, along with some envy, was the cause of his pessimistic thinking and his demons were disturbing me. So, when he called again, I was very busy.

To help combat and release the shackles of criticism and faultfinding, make a note of the things you don't approve of, matters that irritate or bother you. Please don't allow a negative view to dismiss this enlightenment. Look to your childhood, you may be surprised to discover your whispers of the past encourage the culprit who has you entertaining a negative, pessimistic mind-set; the primary source of your grudging emotional condition.

Perhaps you'll chance upon a truth you've been hiding from yourself, one you sense is there but don't want to face, such as a gloomy disposition. Like a cumulus cloud, inky and threatening, a cheerless outlook darkens your life while it rains on everyone's parade.

Dark thoughts create a bad attitude, they sap your energy. What you think now, you will think tomorrow, and the tomorrows to come. If you suspicion this as you, decide now to make the necessary changes needed. Don't put it off until the "right time"—it never comes.

Your attitude is the reflection of your thoughts, attracting what you feel you are worth. Even the way you walk and talk, manners and dress reflect your thinking. A cheerful, confident mind-set makes the decisive difference between enjoying life, or plodding through.

Attitude changes everything, every time.

Does your attitude give joy? Offer solutions? Encourage others? You are your best when you are positive. Not only do you inspire yourself, others place trust in you, they like you, really like you—they sense you really like yourself. Why deal with static energy when you have a direct line to the positive energy of your soul friend.

Hold to the thought your soul is a positive force who functions in the perfect energy of truth and love. Know that every time ego's attitude operates in negative energy, soul retreats – you can claim victory over this wretched culprit, the demon barrier alienating others from you, and you from happy relationships.

The quickest way to put a fix on negative energy is to energize a genuine smile. You can even ho, ho, ho! if you choose. Just turn your lips up and create a happy face. Do this when you're alone, when you're with others. Do it now, while reading this sentence. Nice difference, no? Yes! Feel good? Yes! Do it before dark thoughts give you the blues. With all your might force yourself to think up. This positive infusion transmits to every cell, and now, happy cells deliver a super-charge of magnificent energy throughout your being, offering cheerful, positive thinking for meaningful relationships and outcomes.

Another "inspired" charge to overcome a poor attitude is a sweet breath of life. Do you know your posture changes when you take deep breaths? Diaphragm expands, rib cage lifts, allowing the lungs to take in more oxygen. The increased supply fills the blood stream to the brim, strengthening not only your lungs and heart, but every organ in your body. Even your skin feels and looks better—and even more, thinking is clearer, sharper, helping you let go of tiresome, troublesome thought.

Whenever you're not feeling up to par, don't reach for an aspirin. Take slow, deep breaths, several times a day. More is better. Side effects: better circulation, good digestion, more energy, smart thinking, healthy heart, happy mind.

Why hang on to the negative culprits, struggling through each day breathing a shallow ether? Because you are afraid, you have settled in with fear.

Why live with fear? After all, that's a ludicrous thing to do when you stop and think about it. Well, maybe you don't want to let go of the comfort of past teachings and experiences, however negative or wrong they may have been. This would mean letting go of a part of yourself, an admission those whose example you followed were mistaken. Ergo, you are mistaken—and emotionally confused. Horrors! Let's not give that another thought!

Suppose your dad had a drinking addiction and the only time he'd pay a visit would be to abuse your mother or throw rocks through the windows. (That reality seems familiar to me.) Such an experience may have "infected" you with a fear of drunks, maybe even rocks.

Come to terms with the ordeal and accept it for what it was—a regrettable life experience. You must know life is an endless parade of experiences. Do you really want to look back and see you let a miserable memory sabotage your precious life? I don't think so. Release your bondage and move on.

As long as you hold on to any distressful happening, you settle in with fear of this happening again.

Fear is the father of every imaginable ill.

There are small ones and terrible ones. Fears rooted from the past; fear of the future, of the known, the unknown; fears that cause us to make wrong choices and do the most preposterous things—or nothing at all. Fear that starts an argument at the kitchen table, or great wars. Fear that stir up hate and keep us from embracing each other, fears that cloud our vision and hold us captive in a fearsome life. So many wrong things are done out of fear.

Fear knows no limit, yet fear is the seed of limitation; ignorance, its blossom.

(One could write a book on the subject of fear and its devastating consequences. This has potential among the many possibilities you could explore, for all things are possible.)

We see the children and long to be as a child again. We envy their boundless energy and marvel at their imagination that seemingly knows no limit. Fear is a stranger in their realm. We remark, "Oh, to recapture the sweet innocence of childhood!" Why do we wish to see as a child again? In the deep recesses of our being, our soul remembers when our spirit was free of fear and its limitations, before we learned to be afraid.

We have grown so accustomed to the shadowy presence of fear, we speak of it casually. We say, "I'm afraid I can't make it to lunch. I'm afraid the car won't start. I fear I won't get the job. I fear it's going to rain. I fear . . ."

Fear and hope are "distant cousins". You could also say, "I hope I get the job; I hope the car will start." Hope is positive thought, fear is the negative. Hope is better, to expect the best is the best choice.

Yet, **the worst fear is the fear of your "self"**. You wrap yourself in a bundle of fear, afraid to take a risk, sometimes even the risk of a smile.

You fear you aren't loved. You fear expressing love to another for fear you will be vulnerable, afraid your true love will find another. You worry your "image" won't meet approval—you aren't pretty enough, are too fat, or not "macho". You dread going after what you want, afraid you haven't got what it takes. Afraid of offending others, you fear stating your convictions. Fearful you won't impress others, you say things that aren't so. Afraid you won't be accepted, you copy the lifestyles of others.

Safe in your cover-up, facing your anxiety might necessitate a change in thinking, require effort, and involve risk. So, you remain in captivity, dwelling with the past and hoarding your fears, breathing a shallow ether.

Let's say your dad had an uncontrollable temper and released his anger toward you at the slightest provocation, then stormed out of the house. You would cringe with fear, and, perhaps, "walk on eggshells" until you felt safe again. Now, whenever you become angry or feel threatened, you retreat to the "sanctuary" of your room.

We may not always listen to our parents, but we seldom fail to imitate their behavior. Proving, not only do we learn by what we are taught, we also learn by what we see and hear.

To illustrate the broad extent of fear, I'll reveal a very foolish fear that held me captive for much of my young life.

Whenever the word "enlightenment" was spoken, or I came upon it in a sentence, I'd tune out or skim over, as though I hadn't seen. For some strange reason the word frightened me. This was totally irrational and made no sense. How absurd! How this came to be, I have no idea. But there it was, the fear of enlightenment staunchly embedded in my unenlightened mind.

What you fear you must confront. Had I, in childhood, looked up the word "enlightenment" in the dictionary, I would have seen that it characterized a free and open mind. No doubt, I would have been a smarter, happier creature. I can attest to the fact that as long as fear controls your being, anxiety will keep you from thinking clearly, or even thinking at all.

Fear will keep you from helping yourself, and others. When you befriend others, the ungrudging kindness lifts the spirit of your being to help release anxiety or dread.

Some of my most rewarding memories are of the times I've helped those in jeopardy of losing what was dear to them, or in fear of failing. I've saved birds and cats and two friends from terrible fates. As I look back upon those moments that touched my life, any apprehension I may have felt was replaced with the realization that in helping another I was elevating myself.

When fear of any kind holds you captive, know its limitation helps define your thinking, your way of living.

Until you see why you hold on to your fears and examine them for what they are, how they affect the relationship with yourself and others, however you may try to free yourself of fear, you will find no rest. Once you decide to let go of negative culprits, positive energy can be devoted to creating a sweet, happy life.

Now is a good time to spell out your fears and see the association. How do they relate to past teachings or experiences? Do they reveal a lack of self-confidence borne of too little knowledge? Or, are they imagined, like what will tomorrow bring? Once you identify what is creating your dread, you will learn the cause of self-imposed limitation.

Promise yourself to rise above your fears, for nothing is quite as terrible and unnecessary as fear itself.

Sometimes, **the step-child of fear is the force of will**.

Have you ever wanted something so much you thought you would never again be happy until you had your desire? Have you ever loved someone so much, you knew your heart would break if you weren't loved back? Did emotions force your will to make this happen while somehow knowing it would end unhappily? Have you asked why things didn't turn out the way you hoped and imagined? Could it be you didn't take the time to center yourself to see where you were going, or why you were going there? Perhaps you are still suffering the consequences of an ill decision. I imagine a few of us have had such an experience.

I have a story to tell you, one I'm not very proud of but it happened and illustrates the negative power of the force of will. A time when I didn't know who I was, and worse, didn't know I should know who I was. Though I thought I was prepared, I lacked the know-how and worked hard, not smart. Happily, this emotional experience is buried somewhere in the reject file of my mind. But first, I would like to explain how I came to that time in my life.

Soon after my marriage it became apparent the man I married had a girlfriend. Her name was Alcohol. When his habit was under discussion, he told me not to worry, he had everything under control. But, in a few years, along with other issues, liquor was his mistress still and helped define who he was. We decided to part. In my despair over "love's labor lost" and concerned how I would manage with two little girls just a bit more than three and one, I came to the realization I was now my mother!

I decided to return to air traffic control and would need to find a responsible person to sit the children. When the regional director told me I had passed the ATC test with a score of 96 (yes!), I squealed with delight! When asked when I would be ready to be assigned to a facility and put on the rotation schedule, my heart sank. I had to say "no". I knew how difficult rotating hours would be for a sitter, and for me.

I set my mind on a job, any job, allowing the most time to be with the girls when they were awake. One that would not require an extensive wardrobe, lunch expenses, etc., for I would be on a strict budget. I got a job as cocktail waitress, worked nights, had a uniform and meals. Nine years later, with my daughters older, I was more than ready to make a change. I decided a business of my own would answer my needs and, especially, time to have with the girls.

I invested borrowed money and lots of energy in a salon for women, offering personal care (lashes, hair, nails, etc.) along with an exquisite line of skin care, jewelry, and then clothing. The salon was very successful.

A steady client heard I was expanding, moving to a prime location; she and her husband would like to be partners. She assured me she would be of great help – would I be interested? After serious consideration, I decided this would be a good thing. I could devote more time with the girls.

In less than six months, under the "persuasion" of my partners, I was "asked" to leave the partnership—the business I had successfully established! Upon confronting the accountant I was told there was a "misunderstanding", the landlord (who was their close friend) said my lease was "non-binding". There was the legal stuff and all. A few months later, I learned the business had closed. True story.

Devastated, I took to myself. Now, out of fear of the future, the force of will reared its ugly head.

I then undertook the venture of the manufacturing and marketing of giftware to floral and gift stores, nationally. My thinking was when success of this undertaking was realized, the girls and I would share in the sweet rewards envisioned, sans partners.

As I had little knowledge in this field, on-the-job training is the operative word. I worked "24/7". Able to afford part-time help only, I wore "ten hats" – calling suppliers regard late shipments, doing art work for ads, sales, taking orders, packing orders, bookkeeping, et al. This venture would prove to be a struggle. Stress was my partner, ever there beside me, loyal and true-blue. My daughters helped when they could, but quality time with them became less.

As the months passed, unexpected obstacles brought about reversals, while little went according to plan or projection. Out of fear, the day seldom ended without "my will be done!" and the greater my will, the poorer my judgments, the deeper the losses. I attributed the hardships to the naive belief that nothing worthwhile comes easy. Those hard years were to become the most wretched of my life. I became totally spent and suffered burn-out. My daughters, my health, my life suffered.

The day I gave up I asked myself, "What did I need to have, or prove, that was worth eight years of my life?"

I couldn't remember.

You might ask, "What is wrong with trying to succeed? After all, sometimes sacrifices have to be made. You'll never know until you try." This is true.

What is also true is early on in the venture, a feeling within urged me to re-think my resolve, to change direction and forego this undertaking. For the wrong reasons, I hoped to redeem myself – at this juncture of my life my thinking was muddled, ego apart from soul. I made my choice (and sorrow) and suffered.

I tell of this happening for you to see how easy it is to make the wrong decision and worse, not know the way out. Also, to show how essential to define who you are and not allow mixed-up emotions get in the way of making the best choices—sometimes, for a lifetime.

Borne of fear, suffering is the bitter reward of the force of will.

Making good things happen is absolutely admirable, sometimes courageous; forcing them to be is not. When we will life to happen, we lose it. Simple as that.

When the free will of ego forces the dream we create a nightmare.

We force the dream we wish for in hope of changing our unhappy condition. When the dream doesn't meet our great expectations, we then remain in the "comfort" of the new undesirable condition, afraid to let go, lest we see ourselves as we are, our life as it really is. Now, more troubled within, unsure of our judgments, we place faith in "a roll of dice" and rest our fate in the hands of others, creating even less trust in ourselves.

While endless hours and energy are spent plotting

our moves to make things happen *we lose sight of the gift of each day, the joy of the moment and sweetness of those dear; the happiness of just being.*

One day we awaken to find we have a feeling of desolation. Our memories are empty of the truly meaningful moments of life. We come to realize we deserted ourselves for "our will to be done".

When you wish to change or improve the reality you live in, the need to exert your will isn't necessary. You know with the right amount of perseverance the desired dream will come about, it will happen. If not, that's okay too, for intuitively you know this dream isn't the one for you. This place is not the place to be—no question, doubt, or regret.

If your desire is to have a certain thing but the pursuit is defeating you, or if you are chasing a relationship that isn't going anywhere, take the time to ask yourself, "Am I forcing this to be? If so, why am I? How important can it be?"

Yes, I realize it's difficult to think clearly, especially if you are in a love relationship and intense emotions won't let go. Yet, if something doesn't feel right and you are uneasy, you may be forcing the dream to be. The strong will of ego may be blocking a dynamic energy from entering your reality. Don't become impatient and make your sorrow. Take a sweet breath, access the voice within and let the intuitive logic of soul help evaluate the dream and the right decision will be your sweet reward.

If you have lost your way, identify the cause— whether rooted in the past, the company you keep, or even losing what is rightfully yours. And, with ego and soul working together, confront the demons that hold you captive—throw them out! Once you see where you are coming from, you can make the necessary changes needed, confident in your ability to create a happier you; free to live each day enjoying a better life.

A few years later I returned to what I knew and opened a gift store. Well, more like a mini-department store—giftware, clothing, jewelry, cologne, greeting cards, gift baskets and yummy chocolates. It truly was nice and well received.

* * *

The following may seem unimportant, yet illustrates the damage and suffering one's emotions can do when not controlled early on, out of touch with soul.

On a broader scale, the force of one's will is evident in several life situations and conditions.

The raping of minds and possessions, or physical abuse, are examples of unrestrained force of will exerted by those who are detached from soul and, out of fear, are out of control.

Political as well as religious wars are prime examples of the mindlessness of the force of will, each faction trying to exert their will over others.

The land of the American Indians was overtaken by the settlers of North America — English, Spanish, French, et al. African-Americans relive the injustice of white man's slavery of their ancestors. The Chinese have all but destroyed the culture and religion of the Tibetans. Korea is now North and South Korea. Arabs and Jews have been killing and maiming each other for years. So it is in Northern Ireland, Bosnia, Iraq and Afghanistan, and other parts of the world.

It is evidenced by the radical governing of the leaders of many countries, the inhumane treatment of men, women and children by dictators. The most extreme and terrifying is exemplified by the fanatical terrorists who believe they have the right and duty to kill the "infidels" — those who aren't of their faith, those who won't bend to their volatile will.

Before our eyes we see despair on the faces of those who live in fear of their lives, the lives of loved ones. We see helplessness on the faces of those who live the threat of losing the quality of life strived for. Their countenance reveals dismay, unease; their rosy complexions have paled. Almost all the people of the world suffer the anxiety of what each new day will bring. Before our eyes, we are witness to the violators, the slayers of the dream of brotherly love. And the children see and listen.

This image of ego's mind-set reveals the absence of love.

There is no question or doubt, the force of will is a great injustice to humankind. Yet, the greatest injustice is the force of one's will upon a child's mind.

When focus is centered on avenging the past through children of the rising generation, the young mind is denied its birthright to develop its potential. To vindicate the inequities inflicted on those before them, the young mind is sacrificed, rendered powerless to think and create, never to explore its infinite possibilities. This vandalizing of the mind breeds more injustice and sorrow, certainly not friendship and love. And the children are held captive, prisoners of the will of others.

One may quarrel that the children's moral responsibility is loyalty to their parents. I understand. But is fostering anger and hate, even sanctioning killing, the moral to instill in a child? Is this the expression of love, the way of truth? I think not. I cannot comprehend this point of view and grieve for the children.

Avenging the past by promoting fear and prejudice, even killing, won't change the injustices of life, but will sow the seeds of ignorance and hate. And the children become what they have seen and learned, trapped in the past to pass on the influence passed on to them while their potential lies dormant.

If I pass on to my children the wrongs done to me, my teachings will emotionally influence who they become. I then am guilty of nurturing mindless bodies, unable to reason things out and, unknowingly, they will yield to the vindictive will of others as their purpose in life.

When you are gone, how will your children remember you? Will you leave them trapped in the past to pass on the injustice passed to them? Or, will they know you rose above misfortune to make a better life for them?

The way out is to teach by good works and deeds, so the children can know love and have the joy of giving love. They will create the life they wish for, living on the sunny side of the street in the classy neighborhood of peace and goodwill.

There is yet another will as harmful as any I can imagine. It seldom inflicts physical harm but the moral decay affects us all. I speak of those who impose the care of their well-being onto others, believing others who have earned more should bear responsibility for their lives.

Claiming their "rights", they live off the charity and welfare of the state and government at great cost to the people. Rather than working to support themselves, they will their needs be met. Instead of applying themselves in whatever way able, they will that they be sustained, even entertained. They parasitically consume life's energy like remoras on a shark.

The will of those who find others are not in agreement with their point of view reach for their "leverage", even a gun, to erase the objection that stands in the way of their out-of-control, control – their will be done!

We are bewildered as to why the fabric of our society is unraveling. The deterioration reflects the self-serving ends of many of our leaders and politicians, directors and department heads of government, from the local level to the Oval Office.

Rather than offering to do for the people what they grant for themselves, the politicos, messing with the truth promise even more to be elected. Rather than applying rational thinking to accomplish good things, as expected of one entrusted to high office, their "will" is centered on obscene personal gain and whose "party" has the majority rule. We must pay attention to how they behave, not what they promise—their performance defines who they are. I have the uneasy feeling few give thought to who they are— sorely in need of a moral compass.

How sad indeed to discover those who represent "we, the people" illustrate the negative outcome of one's will over others. Is there any wonder the people of our great America are breathing a shallow ether? Oh! Where have all the "statesmen" gone?

The reason there are so few magnificent lives is simply that man has abandoned his magnificent being—ego separate from soul.

The thirst for knowledge, the passion to achieve excellence, has yielded to ego's emotional need for self-gratification.

Not surprising when you consider for many the mark of success lies in exerting their will, controlling others; or we exerting our will, controlling them. Our lives are undone so that our will, will be done.

We have no right to control another's life, as others have no right to control our life. Once we decide to be better than we are, we find there is no need, or desire, to control another's life. Our self-esteem respects the rights of others to believe what their conscience dictates is right for them. No longer a threat to each other, we find it easy to get along.

When this happens we will have a kinder and happier world, living in the harmony of brotherly love, our beautiful world at peace.

Utopia? Yes, it can happen. You can begin now in your corner of the world.

~~ essentials ~~

We have been traveling over some unpleasant, rugged terrain. It's time to rest. It's time to have some "yum-yums" and bask in the sun.

Let's relax with a sweet breath or two . . .
savor the sweetness, the strength and comfort,
soul's energy is giving you.

Yes, the best things in life are free.

I am writing outdoors amidst the Lady Banks yellow rose vine that unfolds its hundreds of blossoms the 21st day of each March and twines around the post of the patio onto the wall simply to delight my senses! (Breathe)

Imagine! All this happiness created from a tiny seed! **Imagine what you can do!**

Truly, the best things in life *are* free. Yes, they are.

You come to realize the blessing of this day is enough—and you are gratified.

Love Is The Breath . . .

Good morning! The birds are singing their sweet love songs. Are you listening? Good. Have you been taking sweet, deep breaths? Very good. Having conversation with your soul friend? Perfect. You are in the energy of love, for "love is the breath of soul that nourishes you".

* * *

At the moment of conception, soul pulses the current of life into your being through the energy of love. The moment you acquire conscious awareness, you are endowed with free will. Free will (ego) determines the thought condition that will emanate your unique vibration.

Don't you think it's pretty nice—you are given life and can to do with as you wish? Absolutely divine!

Your vibration is the rhythm of your being, the spirit of your soul; it is the unspoken message transmitting the perception you hold of yourself, others, and life.

The quality of your vibration is governed by the values and choices ego has placed in your mind, and the beliefs ego has allowed others to place there. At any given moment, your demeanor conveys the positive or negative energy of your emotional state, thought condition and physical being—the "aura" others perceive as you.

How do you perceive yourself? Do you ever give yourself a thought? I hope so. Would you say you are a pretty nice person? Yes? Does this mean you are pleasant, honorable, interested in others, engaged in life? Or, you are pleasant but aren't interested in social interaction and keep to yourself. Quite a difference you can see.

It's easy to see the importance of clearly defining who you are. Accurate self-knowledge is essential to fully digest any learning, or the enlightenment won't mean as much, may not motivate or inspire you.

So, how do you perceive yourself? What mental hold has ego placed upon your being?

More than any one thing, how you think of yourself determines the outcome of your life.

If you are your best friend and know who you are, I'd like very much to be your friend. If your self-perception is muddled and grim, most likely your relationships and celebration of life will be the same—muddled and grim.

When your vibration conveys self-confidence, the positive thought condition draws others into your captivating magnetic field. They perceive you as a winner, and you expect a winning performance from them. Your elevating example is an inspiration, motivating others to do their best and make the most of life's journey. Their positive vibrations reflect back to you, re-energizing you.

I have a dear friend who is seven years past ninety! She is a grand lady, a great delight. One can't help feeling good in her presence. Her vibrant energy uplifts me, a reflection of the positive relationship I now have with myself. She thinks young, acts young, perceives herself as young, and as you perceive yourself to be, you are.

Does this happy vibration help define who you are?

I'm sure you have friends who are full of vim and vinegar; they seem to be charged with a very special energy. You like being in their presence, their spirited vibrations just make you feel good. If you haven't such friends, this is a good clue your vibration is attracting uninteresting others.

I have another dear friend who is young and quite lovely. Yet, unhappiness with her physical appearance and unfulfilled dreams hold her captive from seeing her beauty and enormous potential. Her tense vibration reveals an obvious disconnect within, the reason for her sorry self-perception. When in her company too often she has little positive to say, conversation then is like having cake without frosting. Her unrest touches me and I feel her anxiety, a reminder of my own misgivings I once held.

Upon some soul-searching, should you sense your vibration is out of sync, missing a beat, learn why there isn't joy in your heart, why you choose to punish yourself.

Perhaps, it's a matter of exchanging lazy habits for gratifying, fulfilling ones, like doing for yourself what others do for you. Maybe, a concern of letting go of empty thoughts and making good things happen, not idly wishing this be so. Until you effect a change, nothing will change. Then, how will you create realities from the infinite possibilities of your magnificent being? How will your dreams come true? Aren't you curious about your potential?

Among the saddest of words is to hear someone say: "But I had such potential."

If you have lost your way, not sure where you are headed, if life is not so easy, it's time to learn why not and have no regrets. You must know self-doubt is a terrible thing to entertain and regret is a sad state of mind, hard on the emotions.

Vibrations of energy can be sensed in a person's voice, over the phone, even felt through the television screen. When the Olympics or games of sport are being televised I try to watch every event.

When contestants surpass them self or players make exceptional plays, then exhibit physical expression of joy in praise of their magnificent being, their vibrations of perfect energy come right through the screen and are contagious.

This celebration of achievement inspires me to be a winner, too. I hope they never stop openly expressing their joy and continue sharing their happy spirit with us.

Those who are happier, smarter, and "have it all" are interactive with their being, confident and sure, without fear or doubt, focused on their thoughtful purpose. Their vibration echoes the friendship of ego and soul, consequently, their journey is happy and rewarding.

Please don't weary of my repetitive message to make the ego-soul connection and learn who you are. The positive interaction will change your perception; your perception will change your vibration. Soon you will discover the secret to "having it all" is in knowing who you are and where you are going.

The indifference of one whose being reflects the thought condition of unconcern is the most debilitating, for it is static and produces no good thing while consuming life's energy.

If you are involved with a partner who is of this nature, whether business or romantic, unless ego and soul are best friends, your behavior and response to life will be affected by his or her harmful hold on your being. You may react in bold ways contrary to your nature, or you may become withdrawn, unresponsive to others to cover up the loss of self-esteem.

If emotions or money, or both, hold you captive from ending the relationship, know you are allowing this, along with your partner's indifference, to undermine you. The choice is yours whether circumstance controls you or you change the circumstance.

Don't forget, you are your choices.

Should you find there is no change after talking it over with the one involved, know there is nothing more you can do. This person only can free their self-imposed barrier of indifference once they choose to. But ego's free will can free you. Take some sweet breaths and walk away. No, run! Run fast! Then keep close company with those who inspire you to be more, laugh more—those who just make you feel good! And as philosopher Ralph Waldo Emerson counseled, you can **"Make the most of yourself for that is all there is of you."**

* * *

Let's pause for a moment and take a breather. Let's refresh ourselves with some sweet, deep breaths. No hurry, we have all the time in the world. Feels good, yes? Yes!

While we are here I would like to share an incident unrelated to our journey, one I believe you will enjoy.

One morning when I was busy in the kitchen, I

noticed a coffee mug on the shelf that didn't look familiar. (Later, I learned my daughter had set it there.) The mug was white with a black imprint of a happy cat playing a guitar and singing. Upon picking it up to get a better look, on the back side was this verse:

Love to eat them mousies, mousies what I love to eat.
Bite they little heads off, nibble on they tiny feet.

B. Kliban

All day, when the silly verse came to mind, I chuckled. I hope you find it amusing, too.

Laughter changes perspective, laughter breaks down barriers.

There is nothing quite so stimulating as listening to the delightful sounds of happy voices celebrating the joy of living; nothing quite so soothing to the soul as hearing calm voices softly echoing the serenity of balanced emotion, a reflection of clear, logical thought.

There is nothing quite so satisfying as being in the presence of a cheerful person whose rosy attitude and caring ways reveal a loving nature. Should you be fortunate to know someone of this nature, cultivate a close friendship for this vibration is in harmony with life and is highly contagious.

There is nothing quite so powerful as the pulsation generated by the passion of love. I'm sure, at some time, you've been in the company of two in love. Their vibrations, or should I say, their warm vibrations were so infectious even if you weren't in love, your thoughts turned to love.

Remember your first love? (The second is okay, too.) There wasn't any way you could quiet the pounding of your heart, the joy of your soul. It touched every corner of the world! Remember catching a glimpse of your love passing by? That's all it took! In an instant you were in a state of euphoria that lasted for hours; from the top of your head to the tip of your toes every cell in your being celebrating the ecstasy of you. Sometimes you'd get the feeling that, most certainly, you might jump out of your skin. **Embraced in the energy of love your vibration is at optimum, radiating, reflecting your perfect thought condition of love (truth) and joy**.

As you learn more where you are coming from, why you have become you who you are, and ego and soul become best friends, awareness increases. Because you are operating on the higher plane, perception is heightened, enabling you to view yourself, others, and life with greater understanding. You perceive the aura of others as a reflection of their passion for life. Your compassion helps you see when others may need help.

If you know someone whose countenance has become expressionless, reflecting disturbed thoughts, whose aura has become lifeless, take the time to be a friend lest their precious days be lost in captivity.

There was a time when I needed such a friend.

Some years ago when shopping at the mall I made a purchase and while waiting for the clerk to ring up the sale, I happened to catch sight of myself in the mirror on the counter. For a moment I didn't recognize the image of me, I thought I was looking at a stranger. I stood staring in disbelief. I didn't fret over the (character) lines on my face; all I could see was my pitifully empty expression. Sadness swept over me.

Walking to the parking lot I could feel my energy leave. I felt like a bag of old bones. I sat in the car for a very long time. This wasn't like me; usually I was forever rushing here to there. But now I didn't have the will to move, my focus centered on the expressionless face I had seen in the mirror.

After a while, I came to the conclusion my image laid bare an unhappy life. The quality of life hadn't changed, but exactly as it had begun – still living the harsh early beginnings of childhood – the only difference I was a woman now, no longer a little girl. The movies (conditions) had new titles, yet I was acting out the same sorrowful script of the past.

Not wanting to think about it any longer, I decided I was stressed from trying to do too many things and attributed the incident to an emotional moment in time. "A night's good rest is really all I need", I told myself. Putting my emotional reaction aside I started the car, not realizing I was holding onto pain and sorrow like precious jewels, not wanting to lose them or to let them go.

I didn't know then, but in a few years my miserable self would come to surface. Almost everything I had worked for, dreamed of, turned out badly; almost everything I attracted became a losing game. I grew despondent, heartbroken, ill, and lived with despair until I learned "I *am* my soul", saw who I had become, and made the necessary changes needed.

You may think you are fooling yourself, even others, playing a game of pretending all is well, but the pretense will only worsen, your vibration will belie the disguise. The message soul transmits will reveal your true condition—seen on your face, the way you act, the words you speak.

Perhaps your vibration gives pretense of happiness while within you struggle with mixed emotions throughout the night and day, dwelling with bittersweet memories of "what might have been".

Do your memories tell the story of a broken heart? Did you give your heart and soul to someone, only to learn your love meant little to the one who whispered 'sweet nothings' in your ear and vowed all love to you? Did someone you care for lie to you? Betray you? Did you imagine things were better than they were? And, did you tell yourself this love could be like it used to be? But it never happened. Yet, the mixed emotions won't let go and you find yourself missing the one who crushed your spirit and shattered the dream. You must know some will take advantage, if you let them.

What are you missing? The emptiness of unfilled, meaningless promises, or the times you nursed yourself with tears to soothe your tattered being? Or, the endless times you worried and waited—alone? You mustn't let your being become captive of another's unattended soul, your life spent in a nothingness of each day. You need ask yourself, "How important can it (nothingness) be?"

What matters most is not how much you love someone, but who you are and how you feel when you are with them.

Perhaps, you believe God has given you this heartache and, in some way, the hurt and misery will make you a better person. Often enough, I've heard someone ask, "Why has God given me this cross to bear?" And someone replies, "Because He knows how much we can bear. He never gives more than we can bear."

God hasn't given your heartache, your choice has; free will chooses the life you will live. Free will won't let go of the whispers of the past. You may take issue and say the choice you made was from the heart and believed another to be as true. Yes, I know, we can be deceived and fooled. But once it becomes apparent someone, or something, isn't emotionally right or good for you, it's not God or the choice of anyone else if you choose to remain.

If you are spent from crying on the inside while pretending all is well, your weariness stems from within, a reflection that all is not well. When exhaustion sets in and you feel you've reached bottom, opportunity enters. Soul, seeing your condition is urging you be still, knowing quiet time is needed to get centered and let go of negative impulses to see the futility of pretense. *The moment the free will of ego "lets go" and soul's inherent love heals your wound, exhaustion disappears.*

Take sweet breaths and let the wisdom of soul nourish your being with love to cure your heartache, for you must know, your soul knows. Once you are one with truth, you become wiser. You see how worthless the cover of pretense can be. You learn to set boundaries before committing your sweet being to counterfeit promises. Your values change to help restore self-worth and make you whole again.

With thoughts on the higher plane and faith in yourself restored, emotions become stable and steady. Whatever comes your way, you can handle. Wherever you go your aura emanates a beautiful spirit, your poise reflects strength. People feel good in your presence; they like you and know they can count on you. The vibration of your being attracts meaningful others into your life. You can count on it.

One day, it dawned on me prior to discovering, or should I say, uncovering, who I was, I hadn't given much thought to my vibration. Oh, I'd know when I was delighted over a happy happening or feeling punk with the flu, but not until I learned I was carrying a "bundle of anxieties" did I have any inkling, none, that my vibration was conveying a message to me, and to others. Now, happily centered and knowing who I am, I'm quite aware of my "aura" and those of others.

Pause now, listen to your vibration. What is it telling you? You're not sure? I'll help. Is your sweet being radiating positive or negative energy, or even, indifference? Do you have a sense of contentment or feel out of sorts, perhaps uneasy? Do you feel uptight, as if the worst is yet to come? Do you force things to happen? **When force is applied, you lose power**. Better to take deep breaths and force yourself to relax.

When you look into the mirror, who do you see? Look closely. Does your thought condition reflect a spirit whose aura is radiant? Or, do you behold the visible image of dark thoughts emanating fear and limitation, in bed with a spiritless life.

When was the last time you looked into the mirror and saw happiness?

Does your aura attract the type of friendships that energize you? Does your vibration lack warmth, sending the message the compassion you hold is of small measure or the love in your life is less than hoped for, dreamed of?

Remember, your vibration is the spirit of your soul, the rhythm of your being, and resonates who you are. Should the free will of ego choose to be joyless, soul can only reflect the unhappiness of ego.

If your soul be ignored, echoing ego's disunity, you will attract faint-hearted people into your life. And should the one you attract dwell in like condition, who then are you loving? Who is your love loving? Where is the substance, the truth? For it is one's "soul" we love and if our souls be empty we shall remain captive in a vacant dream.

If your relationships lack depth and lie on the surface, and your dreams fall apart at the seams; if something seems missing from your life yet you prefer to wear blinders, you must ask why you choose to hide behind a masquerade. Is it fear or false pride? Find out. As long as you hold onto the illusion nothing will change, not even you. Nor will you attract those who dwell in the energy of love into your life.

It's time to change your life and live! Don't wait for tomorrow to come, tomorrow is here. Now is the time to live life in splendor!

Instead of fleeting relationships to leave you weary from doubt, or chasing whimsical dreams with emptiness the reward; rather than emptying your purse to fill the void in your life with "things", you come to know what you are in search of. You see these things because you have removed your masquerade. You have made a necessary change.

Have ego have a talk with soul. Don't be deluded life's journey will unfold perfectly without this partnership. Once they are partners, soul's unerring guidance will generously supply ego with the good sense and confidence to make the difference in your life. When you discover what changes need be made, make them. You mustn't fret over the past, learn from it and have no regrets.

Take sweet, deep breaths. Let the intuitive logic of soul bestow you the wisdom to attract "soul-full" others into your life, those whose souls emanate the vibration of true love.

~~ essentials ~~

At this stage what have you come upon and identify with, relate to? Take note of the instances that stir up an emotional reaction, pencil them out to see what you are feeling, what your inmost thoughts are conveying. I'm aware I have mentioned this several times, but it does bear repeating (repetition *is* effective). This works. Yes, it does.

Perhaps, you recognize a pattern of unfilled promises or commitments made that were meaningless, of pennyworth value. If you see you were disappointed with the outcomes, had you considered the consequence of your actions? Or, were your expectations unrealistic.

Do your relationships fail because you embellish the truth, aren't entirely up front? **When you aren't honest with yourself, you aren't truthful with others.**

Look into the whispers of the past to learn the cause of your weakness; learn why you don't respect yourself and, consequently, others.

Have you given thought to how you perceive yourself? What aura attends you? Who or what brings on negative thinking? Can cause dark feelings? Gives distress?

Please don't just read the words—confront the culprits who sabotage your life.

Like a fortune teller, I can tell you this:

You get only one life to live—only one. If you haven't a clue to who you are, where you are coming from, or why you suffer emotional distress, I see trouble ahead.

Unlike a fortune teller, tell me who admires you, thinks you are the "cat's whiskers" and I will tell you who you are.

Keep in mind **when you fail to prepare, you prepare to fail**. Preparation is 90% of any undertaking. To meet success in any endeavor, you need to decide who you are to know where you're going. If you take the same meandering path over and over again, the odds are you will reach the same end.

Know **you get what you expect to get**. So, be wise, reprogram your mind-set and be smart; be confident and change direction. **Decide now to expect the very best from you**. You are a child of the universe, you can do this. You have the power. And, yes, it does matter.

Take a sweet, deep breath of life—feel it, embrace it. Savor the sweetness, the strength and comfort, soul's energy gives you. And again, let this good energy fill your head with smart thinking.

Your happy countenance will attract like-minded others into your world.

Yes, it will.

A Song to Guide You

I hope ego has been chatting with soul, becoming instinctive; they must be the best of friends—be best friends. This partnership is essential to experience a sweet, happy life. Your transformation depends on their relationship.

* * *

The song to guide you is the inside voice of your soul, universally known as:

Intuition = immediate knowing or learning, without conscious use of reasoning.

Intuit (in-to-it) = to know, or be aware of by intuition.

Intuitive logic = knowledge through experience; intelligence, perception of intrinsic truth.

Intrinsic = essential, inherent, located within.

Hear it again; implant this in your consciousness. Intuition is the immediate knowing without the conscious use of reasoning. It is knowing and understanding that knowing – is "into you". I define it as: **Intuition is the voice of soul calling attention to your emotion within**.

The song to guide you tells you whether you are doing the right thing; if you are making the best decision or taking the wrong direction; if the one beside you is your true love. The voice of soul is letting you know how you feel about what is happening around you, the impression you receive of those you first meet. It is the instinct you sense when fear is present or when you are about to do something against your nature. The song you hear is always in sweet harmony, ever in perfect chord to play the rousing symphony orchestrated just for you.

When we don't trust our instinct, we get into trouble. We create our personal storm.

When I was at the children's home the Kiwanis Club, a local benevolent organization, announced they would be sponsoring a lake picnic for everyone. Since our yearly "excitement" was a few pieces of hard candy in a red-net stocking at Christmas (no insult, there were 300-350 of us), during the days prior to the outing we could barely contain ourselves. My goodness! This was a childhood dream coming true!

Because there were so many of us, we were put into groups according to our "cottage". My cottage was in the last group. As it turned out, the lake picnic was unfortunate for me.

At last, the long-awaited day arrived. We were playing on the shore having the time of our life when someone in my group suggested one of us should swim out to the buoy. Now, this was a very large lake of very deep water and the buoy was a long distance out.

I don't recall how it came about, but my playmates determined I should be the one to accomplish this great feat. I backed off. They begged me on. Again, I backed away. They urged me on. My "inside voice" warned me not to comply. I felt threatened by the thought that if I didn't prove myself, my friends might not think well of me.

I hesitated, then went to the water's edge and began my dog-paddle swim. I was eleven years old.

A short distance out, a rush of fear came over me and the voice within urged me to return to shore. I turned to head back and could see my friends, standing all in a row, waving to me. I didn't dare return to shore now. I felt some reassurance there were others swimming nearby and continued on.

About half way out my strength gave way. I called for help. I swallowed water and went under, then struggled to the top. I called for help and went under again. My arms grew very heavy, my legs wouldn't move. And then again, I went under. There was a pounding in my throat and I didn't like the taste of the water. And why was the water brown? I always thought it was blue. My energy totally left me.

My next dim awareness was that of an arm around me. For a brief moment I thought I saw the sky. When I regained consciousness I was lying on the shore, my lifesaver breathing life into me. As soon as I began breathing on my own, he disappeared into the crowd that had gathered. I never saw him again, or learned who he was. I never had the chance to express my deep gratitude. Whoever you are, wherever you may be, I salute your magnificent being!

I didn't follow my instinct, didn't listen to my song, and created my worst condition. It was some time before I was myself again.

Most likely, you have experienced the pressure of having to make a hurried decision to prove yourself or fulfill the wish of another to maintain a happy relationship.

There are numerous pressures, or threats, that enter our life. Some come from out of nowhere, some are always there. Where do they come from? Why do they happen? They come from the disconnect with our being. We aren't listening to our "song".

An example of a little threat: A dear friend offers you a rich dessert she has painstakingly made and insists you have some. You have been having digestive issues and are fairly certain if you eat the dessert, most likely, you will suffer the consequence of an upset tummy. You also know, if you refuse, your friend's feelings will be hurt. Instinctively, your "inside voice" tells you not to eat the dessert.

If you are in harmony with your song, you will tell your friend you are certain the dessert is delicious and appreciate her sweet endeavor, but must say "no". You have wisely followed your "gut feeling". The threat is gone, you feel good, and your true friend loves you anyway.

Example of a big threat: A job assignment you have been hoping for is offered. You are told you have two days to decide whether you wish to sign the contract. This is something you have long been wanting. However, upon reading the contract learn there are conditions not entirely to your liking. Depending on the relationship of ego and soul, one of the following outcomes will result.

1. Though you aren't happy with all of the conditions in the contract, the threat of losing the assignment disturbs you. Immediately, you sign on the dotted line. You are "out of tune" with your song.

2. You decide to think about this; after all, you have two days. You wait for a lead or a "sign" — nothing. You wish there was more time to mull it over. You decide to take your chances and sign the contract. You aren't in harmony with your song.

3. After carefully studying the contract, intuitively, you know which path you will take. You follow your inside voice, in perfect harmony with your song.

You see, you invite the circumstances that enter and alter your life to bring about the wanted or unwanted outcome. When ego is in harmony with the voice within, the right decision is made. When ego turns a deaf ear or pretends not to hear, you create your personal storm, left to suffer the consequences, perhaps for a lifetime.

Like the song, "Should I Stay or Should I Go?"

Go with your instinct—always.

What reason to brush aside innate wisdom? Why so little trust awarded unfailing intuition? Why not embrace the intuitive logic of soul to be your guide? Well, you haven't identified and let go the culprits of the whispers of the past. Unsure who you are, you listen to the voice of others. Later, remorseful, you reflect, "If only I had followed my hunch." As long as ego remains apart from soul, the still, small voice will lie mute to your ears.

Are you in the habit of making hasty decisions? Perhaps you are still regretting the unhappy consequence of a thoughtless or impatient decision. Have you asked yourself why things didn't turn out the way you had imagined and hoped? Could it be you didn't take the time to center yourself to see where you were going? Or why you were going there?

When you are faced with making a decision, visualize what you are thinking. Ask, "Do I want the reality my decision will bring? Is this likely to add to my happiness, improve my life? Do I want this, or do I want to please and impress others?" You have all the time in the world to impress yourself, the most important being in your world.

If you are listening for your "song" but only silence is heard, don't despair. Sometimes, the intuitive logic of soul is sorting through all the clutter and chatter in your head to find the best solution for you. And please don't ignore the silence, believing this is your cue to go ahead with what you are contemplating. Wait– perhaps you don't have all the facts; this concern must be given more thought.

If you are experiencing feelings of doubt, let the matter go, quickly! This isn't right for you. When it is right, intuitive logic will light up your conscious and out-of-the-blue, you will know; sometimes when least expected and, sometimes, in humorous and surprising ways. Please don't push for answers and force things to happen—doesn't work. Believe me, it never, ever works.

I am aware there may be a time or two when you want the input of a friend to untangle a knotty problem. Help and understanding is a part of friendship, just as you would do for a friend. Yet, in the final analysis, you must listen to yourself. Hear what the voice of your soul is conveying and then, above all, trust your insight, follow through with soul's innate wisdom.

Should you still feel the need to seek the advice of another with more experience, look to one who is confident and happy, one who is in harmony with them self. If you take your concern to a friend troubled by poor choices made, in time you may be commiserating with each other.

Once you identify the emotional culprits undermining you and cast them out, you operate in perfect energy. In harmony with your song, thinking is smart and orderly, enabling you to make the best decisions for living a heavenly life here on earth. No longer in captivity fretting over wrong decisions made, you know what you wish to achieve and on top of the list is the value you confer upon innate wisdom.

At the time I was writing my 'bio' to learn who I had become, I noted my near drowning that helped to define me. Whether I was near a lake, on the beach, or driving with water under a bridge, the fear of water would come upon me – simply because of my near drowning when I hadn't listened to my still, small voice. But that was a long time ago. Now, I am different and no longer fear the water.

Before my friendship with soul, usually when my heart would act up I'd rush to the hospital or, when feeling ill, pay a visit to the doctor. After the happening I shared with you, I didn't rush to the hospital or see the doctor. I listened to the voice within and was shown the way out of my ill and misery.

My intuitive guide urged me to move about and focus on wellness to allow perfect energy flow through my cells and heal my being. There were times when even small effort would take my breath away. Rather than feeling sorry for me or taking medicine, I'd take slow, deep breaths until I felt strengthened and composed.

I'd take walks in the backyard, back and forth, around in circles, listening and talking to the voice from within – often in my nightie, looking like the wreck of the Hesperus. Energizing a smile, I'd say something like, "Okay, you sweet things (referring to my cells), no more pain allowed! Let's let go of this miserable condition. We don't want this pitiful condition a year from now, or even tomorrow, do we? Heavens no! Let's get well and rejoice! Remember the sweet innocence of childhood when we were strong and vital? Well, from here on, this is how we will be."

Throughout the day, whenever I'd be feeling poorly or even somewhat better, or during the night when I'd awaken with a bad feeling, instinctively I would follow the unerring guidance of the voice of my soul urging me to think good outcomes and "let the sunshine in".

You might ask, "Do you think it wise to move about so when ill? Really, wouldn't that be a foolish thing to do?" Not easy, nor foolish—does require discipline and desire.

I now had the intuitive sense if I wished to change my condition, I would accomplish this by changing my thinking and *reason things out*. When the free will of ego makes the conscious decision to unite with soul and achieve desired outcomes, discipline comes as natural as taking sweet, deep breaths. **Without discipline, desire will take you just so far, but not far enough, or very long**.

My despairing health was the result of a lifetime of stress – stress that had created heart palpitations, TIA's (mini-strokes with no *apparent* residual), ectopic surgery, broken bones, a suffering abdominal condition that hurt whether I ate or not, mal-absorption—and exhaustion.

Well, more like a breakdown. Often, I'd find myself under the covers with my arms cradled about me—to hush the mental turbulence, I suppose. Now, I am a different me.

Before we continue, I'd like to share some truths I've learned that come to the rescue when dealing with illness.

Anytime you are in crisis, your being experiencing pain, thinking each breath will be your last, the defining moment may be having the presence of mind to take slow, deep breaths to calm your emotions and overcome the fear of what might be happening. Take slow, deep breaths and say, "I'm okay, I know everything is good."

You may be thinking this would be a difficult thing to do during a terrifying, seemingly endless moment, but truly the difficulty lies in remembering to breathe slowly, deeply. This is another reason to make sweet, deep breaths your everyday habit until it becomes first nature, thus greatly lessening the possibility of panic overtaking you. There is no doubt taking slow, deep breaths does calm you.

When viewing television or reading magazines, try not to let current medical reports alarm you into thinking you may have an illness, or the pharmaceutical ads have you believing you must consume their drugs to experience optimal health. Don't allow the ads to define who you are. (I do believe reflexology helps to energize our cells and recommend *Body Reflexology* by the late Mildred Carter.)

Remember, your cells have ears and listen and respond accordingly. Imagine the positive attitude, the good vibrations we all would have if the ads promoted doses of happy, healthy thoughts for well-being. Believe every cell in your being is well and they will perform as expected to perform. Your being is one entity and as you think you are, your being *is*—each moment of every day of your life.

If you suffer with grief over the loss of a loved one, or are deeply troubled over violation of your being of any kind, know your soul sees your sad condition and feels your pain. Loss of a loved one forever changes you; loss of any kind becomes a part of you. Yet, when thoughts are wholly engaged with the heartache you bear, remorse becomes the very barrier to wellness and happiness. The song to guide you goes unheard, silenced by concern over the hurtful condition in your life.

Am I saying it does little good to console your self with tears and seek comfort within? No. **Our emotions are as natural as the cycle of life and without emotion we would be robots, without a soul**. Though the memory may linger on, if not checked, grief will forever hold you a captive, suffering all by yourself. Time heals all wounds; this is the natural way of soul.

Hiding from reality with sorrowful thoughts will give no solace; dwelling on any adversity will seize your being to attract more ill upon you. Recovery waits through the healing energy of soul's inspiration and love to give you strength and comfort, renewal. And it will, know that it will.

* * *

Let's continue on our way. I'd like to introduce you to an acquaintance in harmony with his "song." It was clear he knew where he was going and how to get there to meet success.

Some years ago I met a man, an electrician by trade, and I would guess, in his thirties. He told me he had designed a house and his dream was to build the house in a certain area of town that "keeps calling my name". His bigger dream was to become a home builder and developer. Since his earnings were taken up for his family of five, he was considering working extra jobs to make his dream a reality.

About a year later, he was on cloud nine. He said he had risked all to purchase the lot he had his eye on and the loan for building materials had been approved. He promised when his dream home was finished, I'd be given a personal tour.

Time passed, he made good on his promise. The home he designed and built was outstanding. I believe I was as proud of him as he was of himself. Evidently a local developer shared my sentiment for he offered my friend the position of assisting in the design and construction of a large tract of custom homes.

I haven't seen my electrician friend of late, but by newspaper accounts he is now a respected home builder. He listened to and followed the rhythm of his song. He knew who he was, defined his goal, explored his possibilities to get there, and realized the fulfillment of his heart's desire, his "dream".

The things you find yourself thinking about you should explore, for where your "dream" lies rests your happiness and fortune.

The voice of your soul (who knows your fears, dreams, and secrets) is urging you to pay attention to your daydreaming, knowing this direction is the golden opportunity to glorify your life and make glad your soul.

The intuitive logic of soul sees beyond your vision, goes beyond your imaginings. Soul has considered your temperament and creative need, confirmed your best abilities, and along with the experiences of your lifetime has computed these findings to assess where your exceptional talents lie.

If you find your thoughts returning to a particular endeavor you'd like to try or a special place you're longing to be, yet are fearful of taking the risk, one day you will awaken to find your dream has died, and for the rest of your life you will ponder "what might have been".

I think Shakespeare said it best: *"Go to your bosom; knock there, and ask your heart what it doth know."*

What is the voice of soul whispering to you? Are you listening? Are your emotions telling you this is, or isn't, the place for you to be? Are you content where you are, doing what you are doing? Do you know?

What was your heart's desire? Do you remember?

If you 'go to your bosom and knock there' yet there is no response, perhaps the silence you hear is the separation of ego and soul. Maybe, too many distractions of little substance have taken priority or the clutter in your surroundings is getting in the way, creating confusion in your head. Muddled thinking is the barrier blocking the wisdom of soul to pass through.

You say you would like your life to be different, you need "something more", but unsure what "it" is, you remain in captivity with whispers of the past, in the static energy of limitation, settled-in with an unfulfilled dream. If you are uncertain of your heart's true desire, how will you create the life you think you want, or know how good your life can be? Think about it. And trust your feelings.

Always, without exception, trust your feelings, for what you intuitively sense is true.

Before I knew how vital it was to literally define who I am, for the most part, my life was a succession of grade "B" movies (or less) with me playing the role of the sorrowful star and each movie ending in great disappointment. After my last movie, I was faced with obligations incurred during the time I had been without an income. My new movie would begin in the red. I didn't like the thought of being beholden, but I was okay; I had no fear about the future.

I went about doing the things that must be done while my intuitive voice was urging me to write and help others fulfill their soul's need to experience happiness.

This time the script was written by a happier and wiser, self-respecting lady in harmony with her being. Often, the thoughts expressed within these pages would flow from soul's unerring guidance into my consciousness. Everything fell into place as I was led in this direction.

There were times I would say to my soul, "Why are you compelling me to write, you know how difficult this is for me." Painful is more accurate. Intimidated by the blank sheet of paper before me, unsure of how or where to begin, often I would find myself in "alpha wave" senselessly gazing out the window or into space. Sometimes, I'd simply have a "meltdown" and toy with the thought that perhaps my soul and I should reconsider the course taken.

Since I never had formal training in writing, I never dreamed I could write anything more than a letter. I had to literally learn the fundamentals of English all over again. Not until I had reached a higher level did I clearly understand what my intellect was conveying.

Upon reaching the next level, constructing sentences that made sense became less difficult. And, often enough, my inside voice would get in bed with me to tell me what I wanted to say!

There I was gathering knowledge, learning to express my thoughts in writing, while listening to the classics for such is manna for my soul. Each concept, so new to my old way of thinking, came through the intuitive logic and inspiration of my soul as I instinctively knew this was the place I was to be at this time of my life.

Hallelujah! At last! I was where I was supposed to be—without doubt and fear or threat. No more limitations, no sorrowful roles for me. Such a happy ending!

You can take your life to a new dimension this instant...

Take a sweet, deep breath. Get centered. Let the conscious knowledge of ego and the intuitive logic of soul work together. As you learn to trust your feelings, your hunches, faith in your still, small voice becomes first nature. Now in sweet harmony, instinctively, you follow intuition to be in the place perfect for you; the place where your heart's true desire comes true. You are in-to-it. Perfect!

~~ essentials ~~

What are you uncovering about you? Have you seen what lies hidden beneath the surface? So much there you aren't the person you wanted to become? Until you identify the emotions holding you captive and toss them out, the life you dream of will remain but a dream.

You say, "I wish my life were different" and promise you will make it happen. Yet, the next day, month or year passes, you are saying this again—and nothing changes.

You fail in your objective and conveniently remind yourself, "It's not in the cards, wasn't meant to be." So you remain in "comfort" with the emotional angst of the mental place you are in and have the right to be sad.

Now is the time to *study* your 'bio'. Read between the lines to learn what shackles you. You may be surprised by what you find "under cover".

Once the demons are identified, you can reprogram your thinking and make the necessary changes. Then, seeing through new eyes, consciously follow through, everyday, until you have it right.

And now is the time to play detective.

What work do you like best? What is your plan, your goal? **Where lies your interest? When you lose interest, you become uninteresting.** Work is a privilege. Work energizes your mind, feeds your body, uplifts your spirit; makes you feel like you are king and life is worthwhile.

Make a list of what you enjoy doing the most. Self-confidence is the key. When you are confident doing what you are doing, you are at your best. Here lies an answer to what "course" to take. Don't be lazy to think about some other time—another time seldom comes.

If your wish is to be "somebody," be specific and follow through. You don't all the time in the world on this one.

What would be your happiness? **What makes you happy? Do you know?** You say, "I just want to be happy."

Do you have a clear idea of what this requires? What do you envision? What would it take to make you happy? Find out.

Before you can find happiness, you need to know what it represents to you; word by word you must learn what "happy" means to you.

Pay attention to your emotions, listen to what your inside voice is conveying. Be truthful to yourself. Once you have analyzed it, decide to bury the negative emotional whispers and you will succeed.

Once you decide you've had enough unhappiness, you realize how much better you do when you reason things out.

To create all you imagine you want your life to be— decide who you are, how far you want to go, and you will know the course to take. Then know the highest point, the best part of your life is still to come.

Yes, it will.

Think quiet. Let go of what you're thinking; put your emotions to rest. In quiet, you are conscious of your soul's vibration. You are one with the presence in your mind. Take a sweet deep breath and slowly, let it go. Again, take a sweet breath. Savor the sweetness, strength and comfort, this perfect energy gives as it passes through your being. Once more, access the source within, "I honor you, my soul, my breath of life, you fill me with great joy. I sense a wondrous change within, and I am inspired. I create, I love, I rejoice!"

Stay the moment in the comfort of soul's embrace.

The Absolute Energy of Love

Are you thinking up? Good! You are making the right choice for creating good outcomes. Are you learning more about you? I hope so. Is what you see wonderful? I must say, "That is wonderful!" Now, take a sweet breath or two—visit with your soul friend, absolutely necessary to inspire you.

* * *

"Hmm," you may be thinking, "the *absolute energy of love* sounds pretty awesome to me — I'm not sure I understand its meaning — explain, please."

This really is quite simple. If I can understand, so can you.

We know the absolute energy of any work or thing is the consummate creative energy of that thing– number one, numero uno, top priority. If absolute energy is creative energy, what then is love?

Ah, love! The sweet mystery of life! Love that stirs our soul to reach for the stars, love that incites our spirit to make the impossible dream come true, love that vows all love to another. What is this love that arouses our passion and permeates our being with wonderful, glorious feelings? Why are we filled with intense desire to make love? What is this thing called love that has the power to alter our reality? It is truth. Love is truth.

The absolute energy of love is: the creative energy of truth.

I knew you would understand and am happy you asked me to explain. Anytime you find a concept perplexing, make it a priority to un-muddle the confusion and have its meaning defined. Remember, knowledge gathered gathers self-esteem.

Your purpose in life is to create. Whether to bring about a better life, construct a work of art, or procreate your magnificent being, this is life's design and purpose.

Your constancy of purpose to fulfill your heart's desire is the energy of your truth. Those wonderful feelings you experience when you are in love come from your being expressing its truth. Surrender to the glory of love affirms your allegiance. **In the absolute energy of love, you create your condition of truth**.

The universal energy of life is a moving force that can be good or destructive, but it must continuously create to be. This is its purpose. If you are to be a part of this beautiful world and live it, you must create to be. Like the moving force of life, creations can be good or destructive.

When there is a flaw, an untruth in your thinking, the thrust of energy will be negative, may even be destructive. When ego and soul are as one, creative energy functions on the higher plane through the energy of love, truth, and the result is positive and good. Your balance and harmony awaken the potential within, energizing you to create great things.

Because you are endowed with free will, **the choice is yours to create or not create**. When you choose not to, the inertia contradicts life's purpose causing all sorts of ill—mental or physical—to enter and weaken your being. Your cells are at a disadvantage here.

Knowing creativity is life's purpose, their mission is to keep you well and strong and energize you to create. Now, under stress, fearful of being destroyed, they concentrate on healing your ill while the untapped possibilities of your magnificent being lie dormant.

Perhaps you have tried creating but your visions turned out to be less than hoped for; consequently, you believe you lack imagination. Please erase the self-defeating thought.

We all have potential—it is within, waiting.

If I or others visualize for you, we will be happier and smarter, but how will you ever know what your magnificent mind is capable of conceiving and imagining?

Yes, it does take energy and perseverance; this is what life is all about. Life is motion, a constant moving force of energy creating energy creating energy.

In this moment of time and space when computers are doing your thinking, changing your perceptions, and electronic devices are supplying your experiences, it is "essential" to have the acuity to sort garbage from good. This is what creativity does – gives you the cutting edge.

If you have little desire and find you'd rather do nothing, it's quite certain apathy and self-doubt, your truth, hold you captive and help define who you are. Whether your lack of interest stems from a broken heart of a romance gone sour, the loss of a loved one, a poor attitude, or out of frustration with a humdrum life—until you initiate and "give life" to something, your truth cannot set you free.

The moment you let go of emptiness and create, you rise to a higher level where imagination knows no boundary to embrace fulfillment and joy.

When you help to build a better environment for all creatures, the interaction with nature helps maintain the balance and harmony of the world. There is more to life than consuming life. Give back to universal energy the energy it gives to you.

You can't help but get a "high" when you are creating, for you are expressing truth through love. Whether you are baking a cake (a "scratch" cake is best), planting an enchanted garden or building a tree house, brainstorming a new idea or re-thinking an old one to find a better solution, you are creating. Even a loving hug "embodies" your truth. Hmm, I like that happy creation, don't you?

Inspired thoughts create good things; good things create happiness. Think happy, stay with it, don't let it go.

You create what you think.

One of man's finest contributions is helping children to develop their minds to create inspired thoughts, concepts that become great works and deeds, thereby leaving them with a legacy that will direct their life with meaning and success.

The creative mind is a happy mind, ever paving the way to higher levels of thought and as you rise, step by step, you conceive finer things. Each time you reach a higher level, ego tells soul to add the new truth and reject previous truths once held as valid. The "little men" (neurons) rearrange the reference files of your mind. The new "management" affects a different rhythm in your being. You may experience a "high" as your being adjusts to the new or added truth. This takes place when you surpass your previous excellence or fall in love (again). Ah, sweet mastery of life!

There are those who believe outstanding works are accomplished through the medium of a guardian angel. I believe the powerful connection of ego and soul is responsible. Why is credit given an angel when we, ourselves, are capable of accomplishing good works and things? The finer in tune we are with our soul, the purer, more excellent our creations.

Let free will free you and make the choice to create. Once you uncover how capable and magnificent you are, you discover soul is experiencing utter happiness.

Creating is life's purpose, but above all, love is the reason to be living.

Your cells already know this truth; they bring it into being at the moment of conception. Because your cells have this inherent knowledge they untiringly express their love by constantly rejuvenating your being, knowing your well-being means their survival into infinity, forever eternal.

The reason for all the commotion when you are in love is the urging of your cells to express the passion that fills your soul, knowing this will fulfill their purpose to bring about their highest achievement—the procreation of themselves, the creation of their truth. The instinct to survive is their truth, in the absolute energy of (your) love.

When the development of creative ability is neglected, the cells primal need to reproduce in like image takes control. This explains why those who haven't satisfied their cerebral need tend to procreate more abundantly. This procreation validates their being by extending their being and is of great satisfaction for the cells, but not always for the soul.

We are witnessing a tremendous rise in the birth of babies, especially among single mothers. The message is clear: their creative potential is being denied. Unknowing, many parents of these babies believe the culmination of their cellular desire fulfills their life's purpose, not knowing that fulfillment lies in creating with their entire being.

The unhappy, unloved children whose magnificent minds "lie captive in the cradle" need to prove something and this something usually creates all sorts of trouble. As they grow, their troubles grow to create more troubled babies, immoral morals, riots and uprisings, and may even go on to create great wars. These are but a few of the mindless creations of those held captive in negative energy, unable to create through love, and who sadly are lost, not knowing who they are or where they are going.

When the Creator decided life's purpose would be to create, he absolutely made the perfect decision. The great good that comes from creating is as endless as creation itself. As creative ability develops, one good thing leads to another.

Your creativity inspires self-confidence, instilling trust in your capabilities. Your trust promotes clear vision to uncover self-imposed limitations and discover hidden talents.

If doubt and fear have held you captive, logic takes over to supply smart thinking and release your bondage. Smart thinking brings wisdom into view, helping you make the best decisions, helping to differentiate between sentimentality and love and see things as they are.

Your thoughts and feelings about love take on new meaning. The love you give and receive must have quality, be endearing, and as constant as a sweet breath of life.

You come to realize **love cannot be forced where it does not exist, nor denied when it does**.

This new-found wisdom lets you see how easily one can get carried away with sentimentality. It can really mix you up the most. Love sees truth; sentimentality sees only what it chooses to see. Love is not afraid of risk. Sentimentality fears it, lacks depth, is affectation, inspiring false hope. A negative power others may hold over you, a nullifying and draining energy that can control you. Sentimentality has done more harm than has done any good. I'll explain.

If you aren't going anywhere in your career and would like to make a change but don't because you've been with the company for a few years and your boss is nice, sentimentality is the culprit standing in the way of bettering your position in life.

If you are in a personal relationship and find yourself being treated poorly, unable to trust your partner, yet remain, thinking things will change because you are crazy about the gal or guy, sentimentalism holds you captive.

There is a fine line that separates sentiment from sentimentality. The warm feelings and admiration you have for someone, or the strong attachment to the teddy bear you held as a child, express your sentiment. If you carry "Teddy" everywhere you go, sentimentality overrides your sentiment. Your uncontrolled emotion for "Teddy" now changes your sentiment, or sentimental feelings, into sentimentality.

Quite often, sentimentality's close companion is foolish infatuation. They lie together like two peas in a pod. Both are weak expressions of love that create emotional turmoil to sap one's being, torment one's soul. These impostors are agents of misplaced values and poor judgment; they compromise one's very being.

If you are carried away by shallow affection, short-lived passion, where are you going with this? Where? But where you are—despondent and discontent, wondering why there is a void in your life and wishing for "true love".

There comes a time when you must ask why you allow these "companions" to forge your self-worth. A time when you must examine why you choose to play games and deceive yourself, unable to call your soul your own.

How you face your soul is what matters.

I am reminded of a quotation by French essayist, Michel de Montaigne: "I know well what I am fleeing from but not what I am in search of." Perhaps you are fleeing from sentimentality and what you are in search of is love, the sentiment of truth.

If you aren't creating truth in the absolute energy of love you're missing the reason to be living, for without truth you may as well resign yourself to a life of unhappiness. Take a closer look, there's a flaw in your truth.

Take a dose of sweet breaths, have an introspective conversation with your inside voice to identify the culprits that give a false sense of self and lead you to make poor choices. See your life without this ill, the negative power controlling you. Let go of foolish infatuation, the mush-mush of sentimentality. Let free will free you, and return to love. Take a risk with love.

How is the love in your life? Do you create love?

This moment in time is the perfect time to pause and take a breather. Think quiet. Let go of what you're thinking, put your emotions to rest. Think quiet. In quiet, you are conscious of your soul's vibration. In quiet, you are one with the presence in your mind. Take a sweet, deep breath and slowly, let it go. Again, take a sweet, deep breath. Savor the sweetness, the strength and comfort, the inspiration gives as it passes through your being. Once more, access the source within, "I honor you, my soul, my breath of love, you give me great comfort and joy."

Stay a moment—savor the sweetness, the strength and comfort soul's energy gives to you. Stay a moment more in soul's embrace.

* * *

Before we continue on our way, I'd like to tell you a story that, to me, embodies the absolute energy of love.

On a cool day in the first week of September, after official papers were signed, there stood my mother in plain dress, smiling with tears in her eyes. For seven years, less one week, I waited for this day.

On the long drive home, my mother would hug me, then hold my hands while looking over every inch of me. I guess she couldn't help herself. Visiting times were limited and, dependent on a friend for a ride, our times together had been but a few. She would bring bananas for me.

My mother had had three serious, knife-cutting operations on her tummy that looked like an inverted triangle of railroad tracks. When strong enough she got a job and, starting from scratch, saved "every single penny" and qualified for a loan to have a real home for us.

Soon after I entered my new and strange world, I became aware I wasn't like others; something was missing in me. Though I was happy to be with my mom and got along with the people I met and friends at school, a big void filled my being.

Though I'm certain my mom could sense something wasn't right with me, she didn't press. She would sometimes ask if there was anything I wished to tell her. I'd say I was okay. But the events of the day I went to the children's home and the years there were the undoing of my spirit, and had created a robotic me.

I wanted to tell her of the times I had been afraid and sad, and often punished, until I learned to follow the rules. But, I didn't. I didn't want to trouble her.

Like the time a friend and I decided we wanted to be free and ran off the premises, down the highway. We didn't get very far. We were sent to the "jug" and how scary that was! The jug was located in the basement of the hospital, used for those who needed serious discipline. A small room with lots of centipedes but only one mattress and tiny vent window near the ceiling. The hospital was for the visiting nurse, or when someone became ill or contagious.

I wanted to tell her about the time when my head itched and the matron discovered lice in my hair! I was sent to the nurse and she cut off almost all my hair, then poured turpentine (I think that's what it was) over my head. I do remember it smelled and burned like crazy! I was quarantined for several days, and lived with "taunts" and bowed head for a long time.

There were more "incidences" and rules I learned to respect. I'm certain the matrons and staff were doing the best they could, but this certainly wasn't "home". My saving grace was school. We had our own on the premises, grades 1 through 8. The teachers were bussed in from a small town nearby. They were less stringent and taught us children well. I loved school.

I never told Mom about my experiences and spoke little about life at the children's home.

She would go to work, tend the house, and see to mundane things. In the winter, she'd shovel the coal into the furnace to keep us warm, clear the icy snow from the sidewalk and porch steps to "keep us straight up". She delighted in serving vegetables from the garden. All things that needed doing she did with a happy countenance, everything she did was done with not a grudge. I had a job after school and helped whenever I could.

Often she would marvel about the telephone, radio, phonograph, and such. "What great minds to think of something like that", she would say. She loved music, loved to hear songs on the radio or the "record machine". Always inspired by nature's blessings and man's creations, she was energized to create and do her very best.

One day, calling from the kitchen, she said, "Come, let's have a refreshment and take some sweet, deep breaths. Let's give tribute to our breath of life." A remembrance of a time long ago came to mind. Looking back, I don't know how she put up with me; I certainly wasn't a joy to behold!

As the weeks passed, more often we'd have our "moments" together. Then, a wonderful thing happened. I began to change. I can't say why or when, but like a seed taking root, the love missing for seven years was stirring. Present in the energy of her love, I was learning to "feel" again.

While into this chapter, thoughts of my mother filled my mind. To her, creating and loving is what life is about. And it was here I solved the conundrum as to why her life had been such a struggle.

When confronted with great disappointment in a loved one, her deep love and understanding granted forgiveness; sometimes, to her detriment. Her loyalty to a friend wouldn't allow her to entertain a thought of betraying a confidence or reneging on a commitment. Her word was a promise etched in stone. Unfortunately, some others did not share these qualities.

To me, she was a success. Her spirit enriched the lives of all she met. Against all odds, she created a better, happier life.

Mom, in remembrance, I celebrate your beautiful spirit.

The Seed of Your Desire

What is your desire, the "something more" you want? You aren't sure? What is your purpose? Do you know? Take sweet breaths, have ego talk it over with soul. Soon you will plant the seed of your desire, then see your "garden" bloom and grow.

* * *

Since the creation of earth and fruits thereof, man has created all things. Yes, man, the magnificent being, has conceived, invented, designed and developed all things since the dawn of our universe.

You may want to ask, "What do man's creations have to do with who I am? Or, how will they help me to create the life I dream of and experience happiness?"

I will tell you.

Everything you are reading is designed to give self-enlightenment (since the day you were born), increase awareness of your soul and inspire confidence, to expand knowledge and be intelligent in your thinking. It may not yet be clear, but the end objective is to help you *reason things out* and resolve the cause of self-doubt, confusion, fear, etc. Once free of the emotional culprits that hold you captive, the wisdom of soul enters to help you create the seed of your desire, your happiness.

Let's continue.

Whenever I think of man's creations, I'm overcome with wonder that almost takes my breath away. And a hallowed reverence mixed with joy excites a response from my soul as though through man's ingenious achievements I am elevated.

It's like the awesome feeling when I see a dainty butterfly fluttering by experiencing happiness, knowing its creation came from the transformation of the slow-moving caterpillar. Or, when holding a sweet smelling fruit or blossom created from the tiny seed I planted. And I pay silent tribute to nature's creations and the creations of man's magnificent mind. One has to be impressed, if not inspired.

What do you suppose was man's first creation—the spear? Booby trap? The wheel? And who conceived the first words to communicate? Do you suppose it was someone who had grown weary of referring to a tree, or anything, by identifying the object with indistinguishable verbal mutterings, or just pointing? I imagine this would have been very confusing—even exasperating.

What do you believe is man's most important creation, has had the greatest impact on society—the generator? Paper? And think of the many offshoots that have enhanced or improved on man's original inventions. After all, through the concrete concepts of those before we are empowered to create better, greater things.

Along with the natural wonders of the universe, **our reality is defined by man's creations**. A hundred years ago people couldn't imagine a machine soaring high above, let alone flying cross-country or even rocketing to the moon! Our reality didn't encompass color television or computers, cell phone, et al. So, you see, a year from now, or twenty, our reality will be defined by the newer creations of man's magnificent mind.

Let's spend a moment with a few of man's ingenious creations.

Inventions and conceptions such as: the paper in this or any book, the ink on the paper, the printing press that prints the words to enlighten and entertain. The steel on the trucks, the tires on the wheels, the materials that made the trucks that deliver the books to bookstores. The windows on the stores, hinges and locks on the doors, the electronic register, the air conditioner for seasonal comfort.

The chair or bed we rest on, the house we live in and everything within; the clothes in the closets, appliances that make living easier, the beautiful paintings to fill our senses. The generators to help keep us cool or warm, and those that create motion—the motion we love while driving a car or riding on a roller coaster. The steel to build bridges, skyscrapers, hospitals, schools; the concrete to build roads, sidewalks, foundations; the miraculous medicines, scientific instruments to help save lives, and the many electronic devices to connect with others.

And music, oh! the delightful, enchanting sounds that lyrically express the rhythm of our soul. How would we survive without the musical creations—from Mozart to Gershwin to pop to jazz? Do you ever wonder who created the first sound of music? These lyrical achievements are but a minuscule part of the poetic works created from man's imagination.

To list all of man's creations would be a Herculean

task. Wouldn't this be a mind-opening assignment for students, or anyone? Not only would enlighten readers of the wondrous works of man, may prove to be one's inspiration to create greater works and things.

One could research this exceptional topic and compile a thesaurus on the infinite accomplishments of man. Title: A Celebration of the Human Spirit. Subtitle: A Tribute to Man's Magnificent Mind. Or, vice versa. This is another possibility to explore.

What motivates man to pursue the seed of his desire? What, indeed, creates the need?

Man's lack creates the need, his desideratum. His love plants the seed and this love inspires him to cultivate and actualize the seed of his desire, his truth, for "love is the seed of your heart's desire". And the result of his creation represents his value, his worth.

When man succeeds he bonds ego and soul; they are one. The inherent need of his soul to experience utter happiness is fulfilled and confirms his self-worth, the value he places on himself. His outward value is measured by what he concretely produces. And money, material wealth, or his intellectual, scientific, or artistic contribution to society is the outward expression, or symbol, of his worth.

The settled mind-set that money can't buy happiness or only few are born into privilege, "entitled" to enjoy the pleasures money brings, will produce little nothings for small result. Of course, there are some who profess an "honest comfort" in being poor, proud to be working hard and just as pleased to state they do fine with less.

You mustn't allow the "money is the root of all evil" barrier from the whispers of the past to control and muddle your thinking. This is a fruitless misconception, a bleak perception. If you cling to this assumption, you won't have power over your money or have any money at all. **If you will think of money as tangible energy, the association will help to change your misguided belief**.

Why are people of wealth envied? Could it be the countless comforts money buys gives happiness and peace of mind? Comforts like the best health care, finest schooling, free from worry of how to pay the bills; free to enjoy life, explore the world, the means to give loved ones the fruits of man's creations that express love and give enjoyment. The things money can buy are worthwhile. Yes, money does make the world go round.

Why do you feel good in the company with those of great accomplishment and wealth? You feel good because it is good. In a pseudo way the concrete results of their achievements elevate you. The success of their endeavor motivates you to sow the seeds of your desire. Inspired, you resolve to plant and cultivate your garden—your "heart's desire".

What value have you placed on your being? Are you convinced you'll never have more than you have? Be more than you are? Is the seed of your desire unplanted and you haven't the motivation to complete even the simplest task, like learning who you are to create a better life, a happier you? You must know, you receive what you give, you reap what you sow. You decide how your garden will grow.

You create the life you want.

If within your heart you regret your meager lot in life, perhaps believing you are a victim of circumstance, why do you idly remain listless in a humdrum life?

Wishful thinking won't change your unwanted condition; conquering the culprits holding you captive from the life you wish for will. Not impossible to achieve, nor difficult.

First, learn who you are, the life you want to create. Have introspective conversations with your soul to learn why you lack the motivation to better your circumstance. Resolve to define your credo for living a gratifying life.

This is the trouble, you know. On its own, ego has decided any effort will meet with failure and be but a reflection of its present unfulfilled state. And most likely it will. As long as you hold a negative mind-set, breathing a shallow ether, your dreams will be but shadows in your mind and the seed of your desire will die. As the inherent need of your soul to experience happiness remains unmet.

Earlier you learned as knowledge increases, confusion diminishes, giving clear vision to take action and sow the seed of your desire. Keep this thought in mind: **"The more I learn, the more I know, the more I am."** If you are under the delusion knowledge is of small importance, you won't make it. If all the wealth in the world is equally divided among all people, the knowledgeable will soon have control. Where will you fit in? Will you be as well off tomorrow as you are today?

The more knowledge you accumulate, the easier to cultivate the seed of your desire, and the more satisfying your journey through life will be. **Knowledge gives you privilege to do what you want, not what you don't want.** What a marvelous feeling to do things because you want to, because you are able to. What a glorious tribute to your magnificent being!

Let's pay tribute to the magnificent minds who have conceived great things since the creation of man. To those who sowed the seed of their desire and in doing so, elevated humanity, enriched our reality. To those whose great works inspire us to imagine even greater things—a salute to their magnificent being!

~~ essentials ~~

Let's review, let's have one more session.

Repetition is effective, gives self-satisfaction, and is most gratifying.

When you have finished looking into the recesses of your mind and are satisfied you have covered everything in your 'bio', assess your past. I hope you included your accomplishments and good works to see where your talents lie, and to remind yourself how capable and wonderful you are.

Study your words, note the occasions that stir your emotions with happy response. Then call on these to help you conquer the negative emotions of the past—those culprits who try to lead you astray—toss them out! Yes! Feels good, is better.

Do you compromise your sweet being, allowing others to take advantage, like in "settling for less"? Decide now to be more assertive, and selective.

You diminish yourself when you try to be all things to all people.

Do others shy away from you? Consider your attitude. Think good thoughts; be positive with yourself and others will be attracted to you.

How is your vibration? Does it send a silent message life's disappointment is you? When ego harbors self-doubt, or entertains self-worship, look within to learn why you think and behave the way you do; spell it out. **Examine the role your emotions are playing that influence and undermine you.**

Have you thought out and reasoned what would be your happiness? **Happiness lies in wanting what you get; success is getting what you want**. Don't confuse the two. So, is what you wish for, with all your heart, what you want?

Are you cultivating the seeds of your potential, the possibilities waiting within to achieve your heart's desire? If you suffer with doubt, learn why; see what soul is thinking. Plant the seeds of change, see your garden grow.

Has a sorrowful childhood left you emotionally empty? Release your fears. Let go of negative mind-talk.

Discontented? Troubled? **Examine the choices made; disappointment comes with grand expectation**.

Has regret caused depression to take hold and a dark cloud has become your companion? Turn to your inside voice, embrace your soul partner to help you let go of darkness. Let the sun shine in and create a useful life.

Think of your experiences as valuable lessons, learn from them. If you repeat the same things over and over again, you can't expect different results. Whatever you uncover, resolve to correct the wrongs lest the whispers of the past, like a chronic ill, consume your life.

When you have finished your 'bio', with ego and soul in sync, you are empowered to banish the culprits holding you under their spell. You are free to reprogram your mind-set. How wonderful is that? Pretty wonderful, I must say.

You are free to surrender to love. Love changes you, love *transforms* you. Nothing can give you more.

Prepare to apply all you have learned to sow the seeds of your desire. You are responsible for the life you reap.

You are the magic that decides your destiny.

All you imagine yourself to be, you are. You choose to do or be anything you wish.

Choice decides your fate to come.

* * *

Of the many things you have come upon and learned, the final outcome rests with your friendship with soul. Like the acquired knowledge of ego builds confidence, soul's emotional intellect bestows the self-confidence necessary to make changes needed. The introspective and contemplative conversations have stirred soul's response to give you courage to fulfill your soul's need to experience happiness.

PART V

A Sweet Breath of Life

Inspirational Love

I am writing outdoors and the saucy mockingbirds are swooping down, nipping at my very pretty cat. Today she seems oblivious to their attack; most times she takes cover under a bush. She is a stray who came to my door some years ago and neglected to tell me she was very pregnant. Two weeks after she first graced me with her presence, this skinny ball of fur procreated six in like image. I named her Estré, but that didn't stick. My daughter re-named her Kadoobie, that didn't hold either. So, she is simply Kitty. I see Kitty has decided to go indoors and the mockingbirds are chirping their song of victory and joy. Such a heavenly day!

* * *

Because the inspirational love you hold in your heart plays a prominent role in your life story and if you are to clearly define who you are, it is good to identify your spiritual belief to learn how it governs and inspires your thinking, your emotional interaction with others and life. Let's delve into different spiritual concepts—knowing what's out there doesn't mean acceptance. You are learning to think things through and needn't fear your soul will judge you for thinking.

I have a friend who is quite a personable young man and a born again Christian. He is fervent in his belief in God and conducts his life so he may enter the Kingdom of Heaven and dwell in its splendor, as promised in the scriptures. We have been friends for a long while and occasionally he comes to visit. Our conversations usually wind up in a discussion about God, heaven, and our purpose in life.

We have had some very enlightening conversations.

My friends know I don't judge others by their religious belief, nor do I wish to be judged by mine. If their belief strengthens and comforts them, that's wonderful! As long as one doesn't try to force their will on me or others, how one chooses to believe is copasetic with me.

One day during the time of my recovery, my friend came to visit. He was "happy to see I was doing so well and had remembered me in his prayers". I told him that was very sweet of him. After some chit-chat about his family and life in general, our conversation drifted toward his favorite topic—religion.

Curiously and in a kind manner, my friend remarked, "I understand you had a close call and wondered if your illness had brought about a spiritual experience."

"You mean something like a near-death experience?" I asked. "Well, yes," he replied, and then, "did you see the 'light' or an angel of God?"

"Well, no, nothing like that at all." I could see the disappointment on his face. I knew how much he wanted me to conform to his religious belief, his God as he sees Him, and the place where He dwells, heaven.

"But," I added, "I saw what I believe were pulsations of energy arising from my unconscious state. I heard the urging of my soul's voice 'to breathe' and felt the presence of a powerful energy of love."

After a moment, with a look of bewilderment, he said, "I'm not sure I fully understand what you are saying. Explain, please."

I went on to say, "I believe when I was near the edge, the driving force of my being was to survive and, in my emergency, the power of my subconscious mind opened all "circuits" to stay alive. To do this, everything stored was released to awaken my conscious mind. Fortunately, the right connection was made and my being rescued me. If any of the circuits had gone awry, I might not be here chatting with you. Because the critical contact was made, which happened to be, 'take a deep breath of life', I am here, alive and well."

I paused and thought about the happening, then added, "I will never forget the interaction taking place within my mind and, of course, the understanding I now have. Since my experience, I am a very different me. I realize what I am saying is contrary to your belief and not what you want to hear, but this is what happened."

Excited now, he burst out, "Don't you see? What you have described was an intervention from God, perhaps through an angel!"

I thought for a long while before answering, then replied, "Thousands of people have been dying for hundreds of years. At this moment, the thought enters my mind of the many soldiers who have died for their country's glorious cause. Where were their angels? I find it hard to believe, or accept, that God would single me out, since he loves us all."

"I believe those who say they miraculously escaped death because they were saved by an angel really experienced the great effort of their soul to survive. The angel they sensed was the tremendous energy released from the interaction of their entire being in its struggle to survive. This was their savior.

I also believe the instinctive will to survive is stronger in some than in others. And, in the case of many soldiers who have been killed, their being hadn't a chance to react to survive."

My friend countered, "Then how do you account for the visions of the devout? How do you explain the phenomena of near-death experiences? Do you believe these statements are false?"

"No. Since my experience I think people do go through the events they say happen. However, I believe these happenings occur in their mind. The "vision" seen is the result of electrical impulses of neurons releasing pictures, memories, etc., at a rapid rate in the effort to rescue their being. The light at the end of the tunnel, the relatives and loved ones, the imageries of angels and such, are pictures stored in the reference files of their mind. I think what they see is the result of the great effort of the power of the mind to survive, and what they sense, or feel, is the energy of this power."

"I don't agree," he said. "Don't you know what you are saying, you are questioning the omniscience of God? God is the only one who decides your life. You must know there is a power greater than you or me who decides."

I sighed. "In essence this is what I said, but our perceptions are different and so we each relate to our power differently. You are of the belief God is apart, outside your being, and that heaven is up there, somewhere. There is no doubt in my mind, God, Universal Truth, call the power what you will, is the omnipresent, constant and creative moving force of energy that lives within, from the moment we take our first sweet breath to our last breath. It is the energy of the air we breathe, the ether in the sky to help give light, the rains to sustain the ever-growing plant life—all here on earth."

We had been having our conversation while seated at the kitchen table, his Bible placed before us. He studied me for some time. Then, holding the Bible, said, "Perhaps you don't believe because you don't understand. The truth lies here within the pages of this book. I'm sorry I need say this, but your belief is the work of Satan and will keep you from God and heaven as written in scripture. You won't experience happiness until you accept what is written."

"Perhaps", I responded, "but, like you, I see what my mind holds as truth. Creative love is my belief. I believe the energy of love is the Absolute, the all-powerful creator of life that energizes our soul spirit, our being. As for happiness, I am content because I have a sense of self. I am okay with me, liking who I am."

Walking to the door, he turned and asked, "How can you believe there is a greater power, yet not believe the God in heaven?"

I had to say, "How can you know your God and believe there is a heaven? I believe heaven is a state of mind. It is here, and within."

And then, with a condescending smile, he wished me well and we said good-bye.

My friend and I are friends still, and whenever we visit, (yes, you guessed right) the conversation drifts toward our individual truths.

Heaven. Where is heaven? We hear people say, "When I get to heaven, I'll not want for a thing. Everything will be peace and love." Or, "I'd like to go to heaven, but I don't want to have to die to get there."

Have you ever wondered why we are so averse to dying? Could it be we have come from another place and this is the heaven we strived for? Or, perhaps, our soul knows this is it and doesn't get any better. And have you ever wondered, if heaven is the joyful place where everyone loves everyone, even those who fought and hated each other here on earth, does that mean we will be mindless, without free will in heaven? Inorganic robots?

Where is this paradise? Is it "somewhere, out there"? If so, that is fine with me, but the glorious heaven I know is here on earth. What can be more gratifying than this most heavenly place? Wouldn't it be dreadful to discover we sacrificed life while living it, preparing for the joy of heaven out there, somewhere? Or, the pains of hell? Yes, dreadful.

Don't live your life, blind to heaven here, afraid you might not be worthy to enter heaven "out there". The day someone can prove life is more joyous and rewarding elsewhere, I may, just possibly, perhaps, give that person audience.

Let's turn to the intellect of our magnificent mind.

If you have studied the Bible or other religious

works, or even if you haven't, I'm sure you've heard the heartfelt stories of God's promise and fulfillment. And, somewhere along the way, you were taught God dwells "somewhere, out there" and to visually relate to Him, you must first pass on to the place called Heaven.

Scripture reads the Lord said: "Lo, I am with you always." I understand this to mean the Creator is the Anima, our soul, within. Whether we are learning lessons, puzzling over everyday matters, or how best to celebrate our journey through life, we are to use the brains we are given. If God were "somewhere, out there" can you imagine how tiresome it would be to listen to the endless supplications of billions of people every day, without end?

I also believe the language usage of those who wrote scripture so many years ago was interpreted and understood differently than that of today. I believe the translation of Satan is all that is negative and evil, not a lesser god or supernatural being who dwells in Hell. What can be more hellish than dark thoughts, hateful words, wicked deeds, wars that maim and kill, and such hostility and suffering?

We must ask why God would infuse us with the energy of life to be the real entity we are if he planned for us to live our lives relating to the ethereal, the unreal? Why are we created in visible form if he intended us to be guided by abstract thought and imagery? Why are we endowed with free will if we weren't meant to direct our lives? What is the purpose of intellect if we weren't meant to use our power of reason?

Why is our being, composed of all elements essential to continuously rejuvenate us, which cannot be duplicated or surpassed, a living, veritable entity? We are not ethereal or unearthly. We are real, valid creatures. We are the visible energy of universal energy and the Creator is the soul energy in each of us. It is our sweet breath of life.

We have been taught we are created equal and, in our conformity, we are equally unequal to the Creator. We are not created equal. The inherited variable intelligence and instincts of our genes bear out this truth. *We are created with equal privilege to develop our undeveloped mind.* How we elect to nurture our "endowment" rests with us, individually. We have free will.

Had we been taught that higher intelligence dwells within and when we are one with consciousness of our soul we are one with the Creator, the desire to develop our undeveloped mind would be our great passion in life.

Had we learned in our tender young years (our parents and their parents, too) we are the real, visible energy of love and when we touch any part of our being we touch the Anima of life, our self-perception and that of life would have made sense and not left us searching.

Had we known our sweet breath is the absolute energy of love, the bonding of ego and soul would be first nature to us, as natural as the taking of a breath of life.

Abstract thought, like abstract art, cannot be worthwhile until the fundamentals have been mastered. We do not start life in the abstract form, nor do we attain knowledge and live our experiences in the abstract form. Before we can concern ourselves with abstract thought, we need to accept and deal with our reality.

We now begin to understand why abstract teachings that proffer imageries in our mind and direct belief in our being outside our being leave us mystified, leave us searching.

Since the fundamentals of universal truth are not always clearly taught, while the unproved premises of those long before are usually taught, we go through many needless, oft-times painful experiences trying to return to our magnificent being, trying to understand who we are, why we are here.

Let's call upon our higher intellect a moment more.

Would you mastermind all the wonders of the earth, then create a magnificent being to live life, penitently, with the promise death will bring fulfillment? This reasoning tells us however much we enjoy our loved ones and friends, however great the achievements, our magnificent being is limited, unable to experience utter happiness and the joy of fulfillment here. We are to have faith and believe endless, boundless bliss waits upon our demise.

This logic suggests one might say to their child, "You can go out to play, enjoy yourself as much as you can, but remember, you'll have more fun when you go to heaven because the playground will be nicer there!" If this be so, why live life with all our heart? Why not wait to enter heaven? Think about this; reason it out.

The rationale tells us either the premise (that bliss awaits in heaven) is irrational or the Creator created his creations imperfectly.

The Creator didn't want us to suffer ill and limitation, nor did he wish for us to live life penitently. Why would he cause limitation to undermine his creations? Our magnificent being is created to be joyful for just "being", to live in harmony and create wonderful things, to cherish the ordinary treasures of our extraordinary earth. Why would he create this bountiful place if he wished us to prepare for another? He didn't. We, of our own free will, cause ill and limitation and envision an imaginary heaven. We create our imperfect condition while preparing for our perfect condition "somewhere, out there".

It's beyond my comprehension why the Creator would create the negative energy of anger, hate, envy, jealousy, and like ills. What is the purpose? Are we to believe our free will is being tested? Are we to hope we shall overcome our failings and in doing so, prove our worth to enter heaven? And should we not overcome, what then?

When our broken hearts despair, does solace lie in the imperfect thought that even with our weakness and ills we shall be forgiven and welcomed into heaven? If heaven is life's sweet reward, why then would we be allowed to enter and muddy the perfect condition of heaven? If we doubt love when it is within us, how will we know truth when we meet face to face? How will we sense the joy of heaven if we haven't a sense of who we are?

The evidence of our heavenly paradise surrounds us. The billions of trees in all shapes and sizes with leaves of green, red or gold to delight us; their fruits and extracts to help heal and nourish our being and give us shelter. The infinite variety of spectacular flowers dressed in breathtaking colors, each with its distinct personality, emitting exquisite aromas to fill our senses. The rain, falling drop by drop—delighting us with its musical pitter-patter, and after the rain, the ions in the air smell so sweet as though sprayed with the finest of perfumes.

The menageries of animals, birds, fishes in the seas that give great enjoyment and help provide nourishment. The beauty of the magnificent racehorse, the glorious colors of the peacock, the endless energy of the tiny hummingbird, the mallard duck with his iridescent head stuck onto his fat belly. Aren't these marvels something to behold!

Add to this the snow-capped mountains, purple mountains, the endless golden fields; the rivers, lakes, and streams, and the mighty roar of the ocean that takes our breath away. And isn't it heaven when you see pure white clouds floating through the azure sky? Or when you gaze into the starry night and wish upon a falling star? Isn't this heaven?

I don't know about you, but I lack the imagination to conceive anything more delicious than the grains and nuts, fruits and vegetables, abundantly here for our sustenance and enjoyment. The reality of cherries, oranges, apples, berries, broccoli, (broccoli?), carrots, and corn, encased in appetizing colors of red, orange, yellow and green, to mention but a very few. Oh, what pleasure is ours!

Isn't this heaven? Yes! "What a wonderful world!"

If you wish more evidence of heaven, take a stroll through your garden or any garden. You will see the flower of truth staring back at you, expressing its truth through the energy of its seed, the absolute energy of love.

Yet with all the evidence of our heaven on earth, we still doubt. We suffocate ourselves with the fear we might not enter heaven. We are intolerant of those who don't embrace "our God, our Heaven", the "right God, the right Heaven". We are angry and in the name of God, we engender great terror and terrible wars, destroying our heaven and ourselves. Does this make any sense? No, it doesn't make any sense.

The next time you spend the day in the country, take a closer look—give your natural surroundings another thought. Be a part of it, not apart. Feel the joy of nature, savor each moment. Get lost in the elixir of life and become one with the ordinary wonders that are truly extraordinary.

Your communion with nature will raise awareness to value Mother Earth. The discovery that your creativity and nature's creativity is heaven will give you a new perspective. This relationship will nurture belief of heaven on earth.

You are indeed in heaven when love fills your being. **Love is everything!** Ah, when you love—such rapture, what ecstasy! There is absolutely no other thing as splendorous as giving love to another and having love returned. Surrounded in love, there is nothing more you could want. When your beloved's needs and happiness are as important as your own you are divinely fulfilled, dwelling in the comfort of love, living in paradise.

Love and understanding are of one mind. When you care for someone, any idiosyncrasy your love may exhibit or express is okay; whether you approve or not, it's all right, isn't it? There is nothing able to disquiet you, for you won't allow negatives to enter your realm. You understand because you love.

Like the flower of truth, you express your truth through the absolute energy of love.

Happiness is contentment in your heaven.

* * *

One day I took the time to spell out my perception of earthly heaven. Here are a few of my heavenly confections:

Feeling good, feeling good about myself
The awareness of my soul, of life surrounding me
Giving love to others, receiving love from others
Holding hands with the one who loves me
Planting kisses on the brows of my children,
the infinite joy of their hugs
The inspiration my granddaughter gives me
Energizing in the sun, the smiles of happy faces
Feeling one with nature, walking in the rain
Playing with furry friends, watching them at play
Planting the seeds of tomorrow's fruits and flowers
Savoring the tasty morsels of earth's delights
Listening to harmonious voices, the birds' songs
Breathing in the exquisite scent of flowers
Hugging a tree, lying on the grass
Strolling along the beach, running with the breeze
Listening to the rustling wind
Watching snowflakes falling on a pine tree
Seeing a rainbow, staring at stars twinkling in the indigo blue sky
Exalting in the Meditation from Thais, thrilling to the
serenade of The Student Prince. Mozart
Creating, celebrating a fine achievement

Perhaps you will discover your list is similar.

Writing your list is a simple thing to do, helping to define who you are, helping you become aware of what makes the joyful difference in your life; things you may be taking for granted that are truly meaningful to you. Take the time to discover where your real treasures lie. You have all the time in the world. Yes, you do.

The Flower of Truth

As we look upon the beauty of the flower of truth, its essence makes known: "I am of truth, I am of love."

Truth is (the) condition, love is (the) perfect energy. In the energy of love is the condition of truth. They are one. A reflection.

One cannot "sorta" speak the truth, nor can one "kinda" feel love. It is or it isn't. Either one cannot be uncertain, watered down, unreliable or uncared for. It must be what it is, cannot be anything other.

When the condition of man's ego is truth, the energy of his soul is love. When the energy of man's ego is love, the condition of his soul is truth. Where truth is, love is present.

Veritas est Caritas. Truth is Love.

Love, truth, is the power, the spirit. It is the soul. Love is the "anima" of life, the cause to pulsate life, the force of universal energy, the all of universal law. Love is the balanced mix of all elements that comprise mind, body, and soul. It is the stuff we are made of, the sum and substance, and with every living thing. Love is the power of each breath we take, ever constant, ever nurturing. Where truth is, soul's embrace is there, each precious moment of the day, every day of our life.

Simple. Clear. The words define the animating principle of the nature of man at his noblest.

Here is passage to Shangri-La, your El Dorado.

When ego becomes one with soul you enter the energy of love, truth. The energy of love is the motivation for truth and the necessary ingredient for the attainment of your truth. As long as you abide with soul, inherent love, truth, will supply your finest thinking to take command and conduct your life with integrity and dignity, and create your Shangri-La.

"Truth is love; love, truth." Simple. Clear. When this becomes your credo for living, this embodies who you are, you will discover you have fulfilled your soul's need to experience happiness.

For all things we see and hear, learn and read, are transmitted to soul and influence who we become.

* * *

Our noble journey has almost come to an end. On the path ahead we shall linger a while to partake in a bit of whimsy and celebrate.

Come! We have sweet moments more before it's time to say good-bye.

Celebration!

Imagine...

You are spending the day in the country with not a care in the world. A few clouds are lazily drifting through the blue sky and rays of sunshine are dancing through the trees, the shimmers of warmth lighting upon your head. A gentle breeze comes along caressing you, welcoming your visit. Such a perfect day!

As you meander through the lush green meadows, sometimes gaily skipping, sometimes chasing the quivering butterflies, you sight the low branch of a great oak and take hold to swing through time and space. Suspended, you recall a time when you were small and someone dear helped you reach the branch of a majestic tree. You recall the pleasure it gave and, once again, you feel the pleasure.

Lost in thought of another time in space, a sound beyond the knoll intrudes upon your reverie. Your curiosity aroused, you let go! You simply must explore the source!

Racing with the breeze, you reach the knoll to find it is higher than you thought. Yes, much higher. Undaunted, you scramble up, up, to the top and, once conquered, pause to catch your breath. "The view is different from the top," you muse. "Like life, one's outlook is rosy when taken from the top."

Pleased with your play on words, you call out for all to hear, "Top of the morning, everyone!" Delighted with your echo's response, you look around to discover the sound you heard is coming from the sparkling, babbling brook below. "Hmm, very interesting, how enchanting! What great fun to roll down the hill; I'm certain I hear you calling my name!"

Lying on the grassy crest, you look to the endless sky and let go! As you roll, roll, down, down, squeals of joy fill the air, a testimony of your pure delight.

Landing beside the brook, you gaze into the sparkling water and the reflection of your happy face comes into view. Such a wonderful smile you have, it even dazzles you.

The brook's babble seems to be saying, "How nice to have you share this beautiful day with me. I'm so glad you came." Thinking this is a wonderful invitation, you cup your hands to taste of its clear, cool water. "Hmm, so refreshing and delicious, I must have more."

As you help yourself to more, you become aware of a presence about. Oh, my! It's a bewitched frog sitting motionless upon a stone, cautiously watching your every move. Staring intently at each other, you wonder if he is a handsome prince held in captivity. You simply must free him and go to his rescue.

Oops! In the blink of an eye, he leaps away, hopping into a field of glorious flowers.

Such delight! The flowers are of every shape and color – the colorful blossoms are a heavenly masterpiece. The gentle breeze whisks their scent your way and the aroma intoxicates.

A baby sparrow finds a tasty morsel, then flies away to join his playmates in song. A monarch dances by and flutters to kiss each one in celebration of its transformation.

The harmony of this Eden comes together to orchestrate a symphony of love, just for you. "Ah, this is sheer ecstasy!" you tell your soul. "To think this splendor is ours!"

Your senses filled, you lie amidst the wonder of this paradise and are drawn into sky's infinity. The white clouds beckon you to climb up, up, upon the puffy pillows and dream dreams you never dreamed. You agree, for you are in tune with your "song", your emotions in sweet harmony. Such a good feeling! A glorious day!

Ego has tossed out the culprits that held you captive; free will has made the changes needed, soul friend is your best friend. Such a wonderful feeling!

Yes! You are friends with soul, your entire being vibrating harmony. You access the source within to enlighten and help you rise, step by step, to higher levels of thought. **You create your truth, satisfying your purpose in life. You love and are loved, fulfilling your reason to be living.**

Your thoughts grow quiet and close your eyes to capture the rapture of this moment in time and space. As you drift off to the land of Nod, ego directs soul to store this truth in safekeeping.

The possible dream is coming true.

* * *

As we say goodbye, I offer you this bouquet of thoughts.

I've enjoyed sharing this time with you and hope you have enjoyed it, too. I want you to know your unseen presence was ever present and played a vital part in making the journey an unforgettable one for me.

Most likely, somewhere along the way, through the knowledge gathered and insights shared, you discovered what you search for lies within *you*. Don't forget to take sweet breaths and visit with your soul friend everyday. Express your truth through the absolute energy of love and you will soon discover you are experiencing the joy and contentment of a sweet, happy life.

The seed of my desire is *A Sweet Breath* has inspired you to decide who you are, the path you will take, as you journey through life—undaunted.

Author's Note

The telling of who I am, my accomplishments and related experiences are in this book.

Upon retiring, I found myself doing what I most enjoyed through the years—writing poetry, short stories, or any inspired thought that entered my head.

I decided to seriously write. I studied the elements of writing and language usage, practiced writing simple sentences, and read even more.

Upon reading my self-published book, I realized the message was not clearly written and didn't convey to readers what I was thinking. I took it off the market.

Several years passed while I continued to study the art of writing. I learned more and made it better.

I made the necessary changes needed and surrendered to my soul's desire, my happiness.

You can too.

A native of Ohio, my family and I live in Henderson, Nevada. I welcome correspondence.

www.SweetBreaths.com